REMEMBERING NORTHEAST PHILADELPHIA

REMEMBERING NORTHEAST PHILADELPHIA

DR. HARRY C. SILCOX

THE History PRESS

Published by The History Press
Charleston, SC 29403
www.historypress.net

First published 2009
Second printing 2011

Manufactured in the United States

ISBN 978.1.59629.615.2

Library of Congress Cataloging-in-Publication Data

Silcox, Harry C., 1933-
Remembering Northeast Philadelphia / Harry Silcox.
p. cm.
ISBN 978-1-59629-615-2
1. Northeast Philadelphia (Philadelphia, Pa.)--History. 2. Philadelphia (Pa.)--History. I. Title.
F158.68.N67S54 2009
974.8'11--dc22
2008045921

Dedicated to my beautiful granddaughters Amanda and Cassondra Silcox and Veronica Hayes.
May they come to enjoy history as much as I do.

Contents

Contents

PREFACE

This book grew out of the efforts by the board of the Historical Society of Frankford to establish under its auspices a center for the study of Northeast Philadelphia history in 2007. Through the cooperation of the *Northeast Times* editor, John Scanlon, and the outstanding support and encouragement of reporter Diane Prokop, articles on the history of the community were published biweekly featuring little-known stories about incidents, institutions and people from Northeast Philadelphia.

Weekly Wednesday night meetings at the Historical Society of Frankford became a steady event. Archivist Jack McCarthy, in addition to his regular duties with the society, contributed to the writing of these articles by using his very able skills to edit each article carefully for grammatical and factual errors. His unselfish dedication to the history of Northeast Philadelphia is well known to those who work with him. Jack has promoted a new spirit in Northeast Philadelphia aimed at preserving its history. Frank Hollingsworth's skills as a tenacious researcher gave the project many new ideas and fleshed out little-known facts about Northeast Philadelphia. Volunteers at the historical society Elizabeth Manning and Danielle McAvoy encouraged historical clarity through their inquisitive questioning.

The images in this book have a direct connection to each story. They come from the William Sliker Collection, original prints and photos from the Historical Society of Frankford Collection and the Holmesburg Library Scrapbook Collection. I am thankful to all for their help. Many are rare and in some cases the only picture available from the time that the incident took place.

Each of these stories was published in the *Northeast Times* in Philadelphia and was meant to stand on its own. The exception is the four-part series about the development of aviation in the Bustleton/Somerton/Byberry area.

INTRODUCTION

ALL ROADS LEAD TO FRANKFORD

Most of the articles in this book are written about the history of Northeast Philadelphia but rarely mention Frankford. Yet Frankford is the oldest and for many years the most important community in the Northeast. Early villages like Holmesburg, Bustleton, Burholme and Bridesburg depended on Frankford to market their goods, as well as to provide the necessities of life. Frankford had the largest population in the region and was the center from which all roads in the Northeast emanated.

Frankford was originally the site of an Indian village and was later settled by Swedes in the 1660s. In 1682, William Penn asked Thomas Fairman, deputy surveyor for Pennsylvania, to establish a Quaker meeting in the area. The first meeting was held in 1683, and the first meetinghouse was erected in 1684 on a site now bordered by Waln and Unity Streets. Penn also ordered that a post office be established with Henry Waddy in charge. Waddy was also granted authority to supply passengers with horses as they traveled the King's Highway (Frankford Avenue). Waddy ran his business from his home on Frankford Avenue, a tavern known as the Jolly Post Inn. The Jolly Post remained an important stop on the road between New York and Philadelphia for over two hundred years. Members of the Continental Congress often stopped there on their way to Philadelphia, and George Washington conferred there with his officers while his men rested in the orchards behind the inn on their march to Yorktown and the final battle of the Revolutionary War.

From the beginning, all major roads in the region went to Frankford. The first five roads that ran from Frankford to various points in the Northeast were the Delaware River Road (now Bridge Street) in 1683, the King's Highway

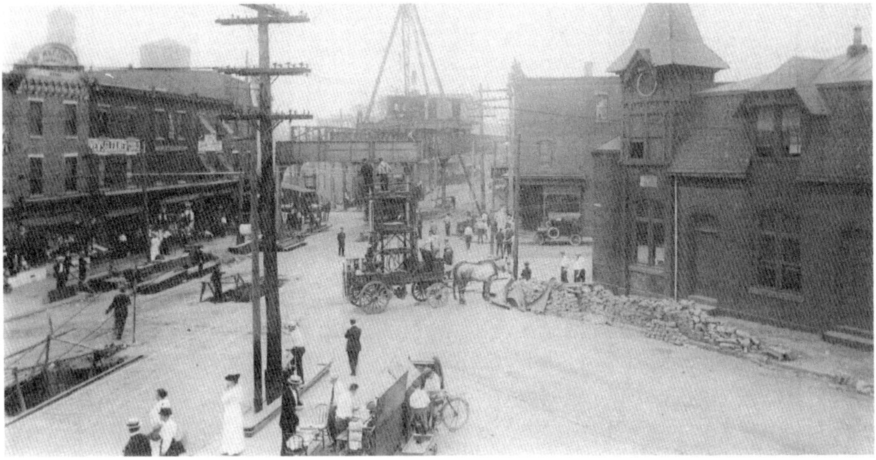

The building of the Frankford elevated at Oxford Avenue in Frankford, 1921. The elevated was the most influential event in the history of Northeast Philadelphia. It provided a twenty-minute ride to center city, which resulted in a residential building boom from 1930 to 1950. Only the war years around 1940 slowed this trend.

(now Frankford Avenue) in 1683, the Oxford Pike to Five Points (now Oxford Avenue) in 1693, the road to Bustleton/Smithville (now Bustleton Avenue) in 1693 and the Asylum Pike (now Adams Avenue) in 1693. At one time, all five of these roads were toll roads that required payment to be used. Much like a fan, they spread across the region from their terminus in Frankford, making it the center of trade for farmers who settled the area. All of these roads are still functioning today as part of the city of Philadelphia's transportation network.

The most important of these roads was Frankford's main street, now known as Frankford Avenue. Originally called the King's Highway, it was the link between the English seat of government at Upland (now Chester, Pennsylvania) and its counterpart in New York. This was not a public road but, as the name indicates, was for the king's business. It grew out of a trail used by the Lenni-Lenape Indians in going to their northern hunting grounds. Paralleling the Delaware River, the trail avoided the tidal waters of area creeks by using creek crossings that could be waded. Originally only wide enough for foot or horseback, the path was inadequate for use by carts or carriages. William Penn successfully petitioned the court at Upland to widen the road "for easier passage of carts and carriages from the Schuylkill to Neshaminy." With this improvement, the trail became the King's Highway, still for official business and still a rough road. After the Revolution, it was renamed Bristol Pike and then, later, Frankford Avenue.

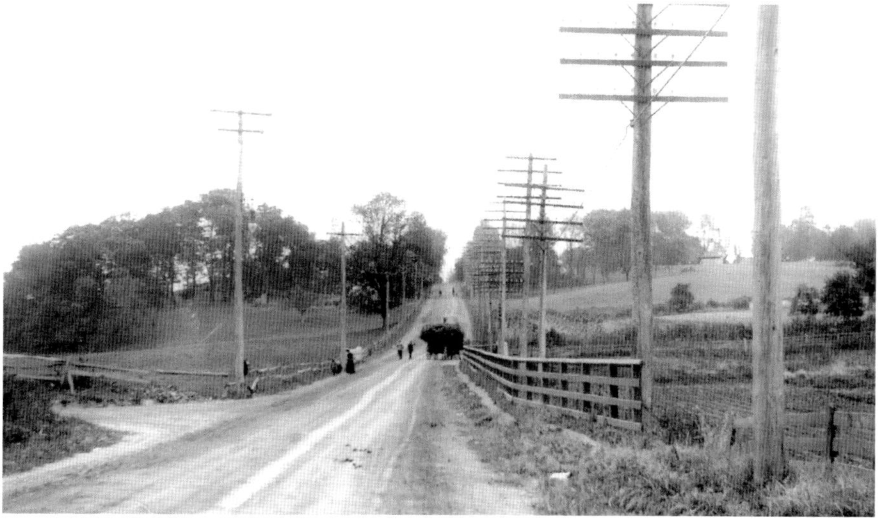

View of Bustleton Avenue leading up the hill to Welsh Road and the village of Bustleton in the 1920s.

The first stagecoach service for public use was established in 1756 along the King's Highway between Philadelphia and New York, the trip taking three days each way. This service, requiring rest stops for passengers and horses, eventually gave rise to taverns at convenient distances that, in turn, led to the development of settlements around them. One of the most famous of these road stops was the Red Lion Inn at the King's Highway and Poquessing Creek. Used by men like John Adams and Paul Revere, it was one of the favored spots for the travelers of the day. The Jolly Post, some ten miles down the road, was another popular stop.

Another important road was the Bustleton Pike, laid out in 1697 by John Harper, a Quaker who had arrived with William Penn. The pike became known as the Philadelphia-Newton Highway, or the Great Highway because of the great distance it covered. At first, it extended to the Buck Hotel in Festerville, but by 1795 it ran to Churchville, Bucks County. It was used by Washington's army when they attacked the British at Trenton because it went all the way to the banks of the Delaware River near Trenton. In 1804, when a turnpike company was started, the road was extended to Richboro. It became known as the Bustleton/Smithville toll road. In the 1840s, it became known as the Bustleton/Somerton Turnpike. Today it is simply Bustleton Avenue.

The most traveled road going northwest from Frankford was Oxford Pike. It was used primarily by farmers to transport their goods to Frankford. It was a winding road that followed the contours of the farms in Oxford Township

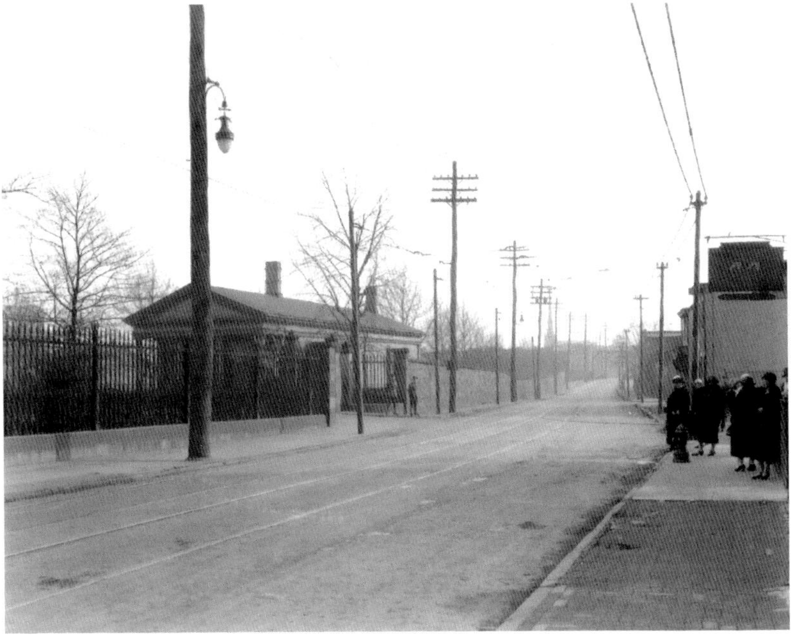

Looking east on Bridge Street toward Bridesburg, with the gate to Frankford Arsenal on the left, 1930.

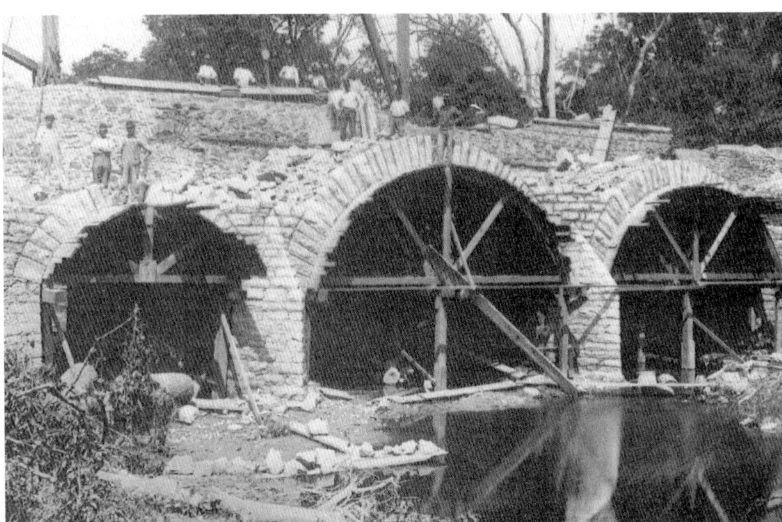

View of the Frankford Avenue Bridge over the Pennypack Creek being enlarged in the 1920s to allow for double trolley tracks on Frankford Avenue. The bridge remains today the oldest stone arch bridge still in use in America. It was built by the farmers of Lower Dublin Township in 1697.

and eventually became a toll road, thus the name Oxford Pike. Toll roads were important in the colonial period because they were kept open in the rainy season by work crews paid to fill holes and repair storm damage. These were generally the most needed roads by farmers because they could be relied upon to take produce to market. The toll gates for Oxford Pike were at Rising Sun and Oxford Avenues, now the Five Points intersection in Burholme, with a second one located at Oxford Circle at Roosevelt Boulevard (the boulevard was not opened to Rhawn Street until after 1914).

Asylum Road (Adams Avenue), which left Frankford going directly west from the village, permitted farmers in that area to connect to the markets in Frankford. In 1813, the Quakers were looking for a location for a hospital for the mentally ill; they settled on a remote spot along this road, thus the name Asylum Road. At the time, this was also the main western road leading out of Frankford toward the village of Germantown. Today the Friends Hospital still sits on Roosevelt Boulevard and Adams Avenue, one of the busiest intersections in the city.

The road from Frankford to the Delaware River became known as Bridge Street because a bridge over the Little Tacony Creek was necessary to reach the river town of Bridesburg. The Little Tacony Creek was later channeled

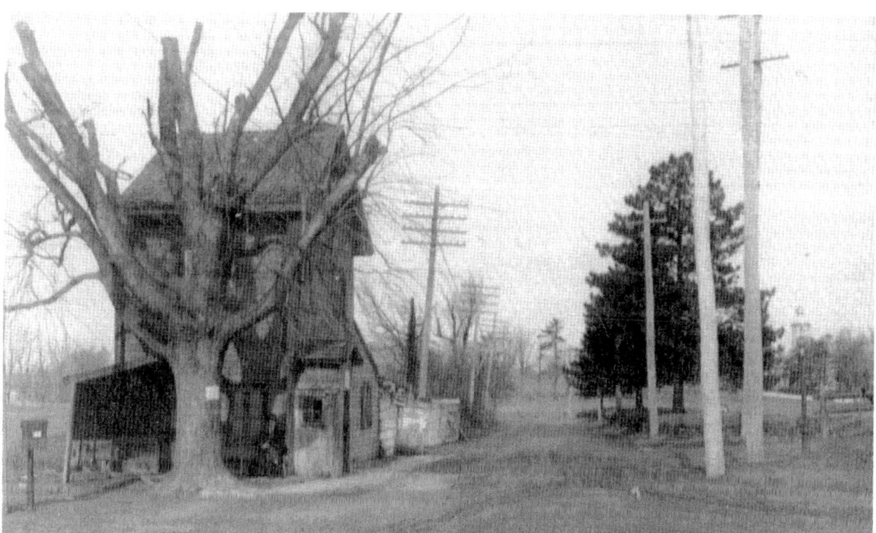

The Oxford Pike tollbooth in 1908. Located where the Oxford Circle is on Roosevelt Boulevard today, the photo gives a clear view of the road conditions of the period.

into a sewer line and paved over. Originally, Frankford expected the Little Tacony Creek connection at Frankford Avenue to provide water passage to the Delaware River, but the tidal creek was often too low and passenger boats got stranded in mud. The most dependable route to the Delaware River was Bridge Street, which was one of the first cobblestone streets leaving Frankford. This became a major commercial route for produce and a major source for household goods coming to the town from the city of Philadelphia. The decision by the federal government to build the Frankford Arsenal near the river in Bridesburg in 1816 made Bridge Street even more important. Many Frankford residents had worked in the gunpowder industry, and now that it was moved to a more remote location, they were forced to travel to work using Bridge Street, which soon became the most traveled road in Frankford.

During its early period, Frankford's population grew steadily. In 1800, the community was home to about 1,000 people; in 1810, there were 1,233; and by 1850, there were 5,346 people living there. It was by far the largest community in Northeast Philadelphia through the early twentieth century. It was also the region's leader in industry and business, with 90 percent of all manufacturing and commerce taking place within its boundaries before 1870. Frankford had its first school in 1799, first fire company in 1793, first newspaper in the 1840s, first trolley line in 1858, first dummy steam trolley to Philadelphia in 1860, first electric trolleys in 1893 and first hospital in 1903. The nation's first psychiatric hospital (1813) and first savings and loan institution (1831) were also founded in Frankford. It had sidewalks and macadam streets lined with an abundance of shops and stores. Frankford's Unity Street open-air market was a popular shopping area that was frequented by people from all over Northeast Philadelphia.

Any history of Northeast Philadelphia must recognize Frankford's contributions to the early settlement of the region. While the Northeast region is today a heavily populated and highly industrialized area, it has its roots in the early development of Frankford. One only has to ride the old streets of the Northeast to understand the importance of Frankford.

PART I

HOLMESBURG

ARTHUR ATHERHOLT BRINGS BALLOONING TO HOLMESBURG IN 1911

During the period from 1900 to 1915, excitement focused on the skies of the nation. Holmesburg residents were no exception. On a clear weekend it was not unusual for the community to experience balloon flights east of the town. Organized and piloted by Holmesburg resident Arthur T. Atherholt, these balloon excursions were the pride of the community.

Arthur Atherholt was a long-standing and respected Holmesburg resident, an active member of the Holmesburg Improvement Association. The association consisted of civic-minded men like Atherholt who met once a month, watched over the health and safety of the town and made needed improvements. Atherholt was appointed to the Safety Committee and the Special Fountain Committee. As a member of the former, he helped supervise street repair and the monitoring of speed for the newly created automobile. In 1911, the Special Fountain Committee was given the task of restoring the fountain in front of Athenaeum Hall on Frankford Avenue. Upon completion of this work, Atherholt reported to the association that the community would have clean, cool drinking water from April 1 to November 1.

Atherholt's active participation in air travel began when he met the world-renowned balloon pilot Samuel G. King. King had moved to Philadelphia in 1906 after accepting a contract from the *Philadelphia Inquirer* to build a balloon that would enable the newspaper to get pictures from the sky. Early on, the *Inquirer* discontinued the project when the owner of the paper felt that the flights were too dangerous.

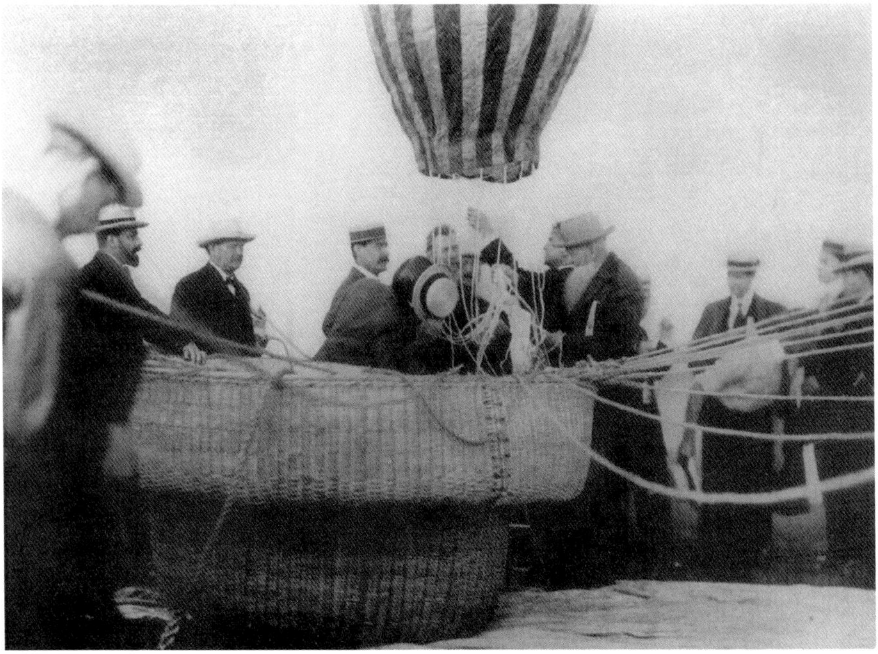

The Ben Franklin balloon basket getting ready for takeoff, with pilot Samuel G. King (the whitebeard) and Arthur T. Atherholt (far left, hands on the basket).

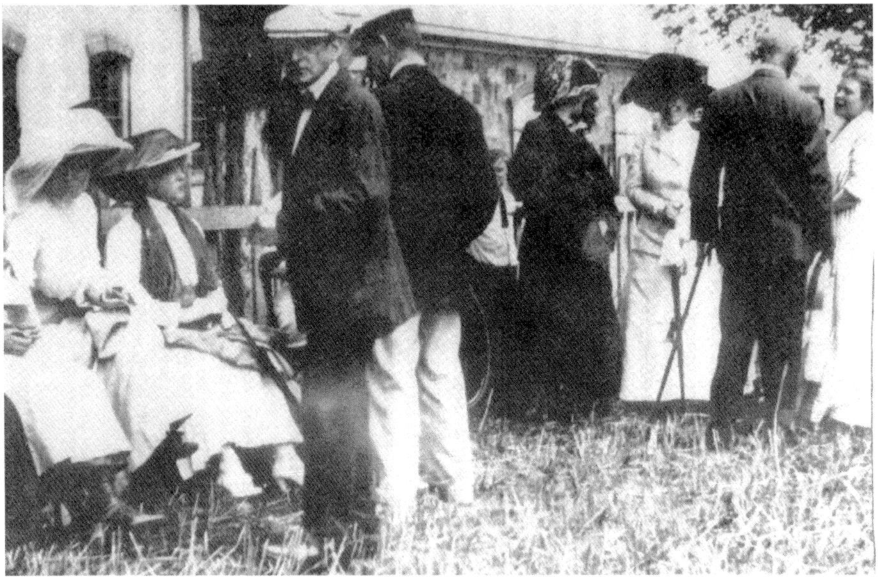

A group of Holmesburg residents at the house of correction await a flight of the Ben Franklin balloon. This 1912 scene was typical of a special event in Holmesburg.

Disappointed but not dismayed, King contacted some former passengers and organized the Ben Franklin Balloon Club. His intention was to build a large balloon that could hold eight men in the basket per flight. One of the first men approached was his former student Arthur Atherholt, a pottery commission merchant from Holmesburg. King liked Atherholt's enthusiasm and willingness to learn the principles of flight. Among the other six men recruited for the crew was William Nicholson Jennings, the foremost aerial photographer in America. Jennings and Atherholt became close friends, the former visiting Holmesburg to take a series of community pictures.

On August 25, 2007, the yellow-striped Ben Franklin ballon took one of its most celebrated flights, going from Philadelphia to New Egypt, New Jersey, in just six hours. Jennings took a number of pictures for the *Philadelphia Inquirer* with the help of balloonmate Arthur Atherholt. Once the balloon had climbed to a height of one mile, Jennings decided to take a snapshot of a christening ceremony then taking place inside the balloon. As Jennings leaned out into space to get his camera focused, he called to Atherholt to sit on his legs to keep him from falling out of the balloon. Jennings remembers Atherholt's face turning chalk white with fright as he sat on his legs. Jennings's only response was a big smile.

The story of the flight in the *Philadelphia Inquirer* was read by many people in Holmesburg. They were proud that a hometown resident was part of the race for flight. Even more exciting were Atherholt's efforts to organize balloon flights next to the house of correction on State Road near Rhawn Street. Gas from the house of correction was needed to fill the balloon. Horse-drawn wagons filled with the deflated Ben Franklin balloon attracted crowds of young people as it was moved to the site. The balloon, the Pennsylvania, made its first ascent on May 26, 1911, with the help of the inmates at the house of correction. Inmates held the balloon in place while it was filled with gas and launched it when requested by passengers Atherholtz, C.P. Wayne and William Sedwick. A picture of the site still remains, showing Holmesburg residents gathered to watch the balloon ascension.

Atherholt became the first man in Pennsylvania to receive a pilot's license from the Aero Club of America. Between 1910 and 1913, he took part in three international races for the prestigious Gordon Bennett trophy awarded for the longest flight. He participated in many national races throughout the United States while attempting to qualify for international races. This national exposure led to his being elected president of the Aero Club of America. As part of his responsibility as president of the Aero Club, Atherholt was invited to Germany for an international meeting.

While in Germany, Atherholt thought he might try a flight even though he was unfamiliar with the geography and the region's wind currents. With

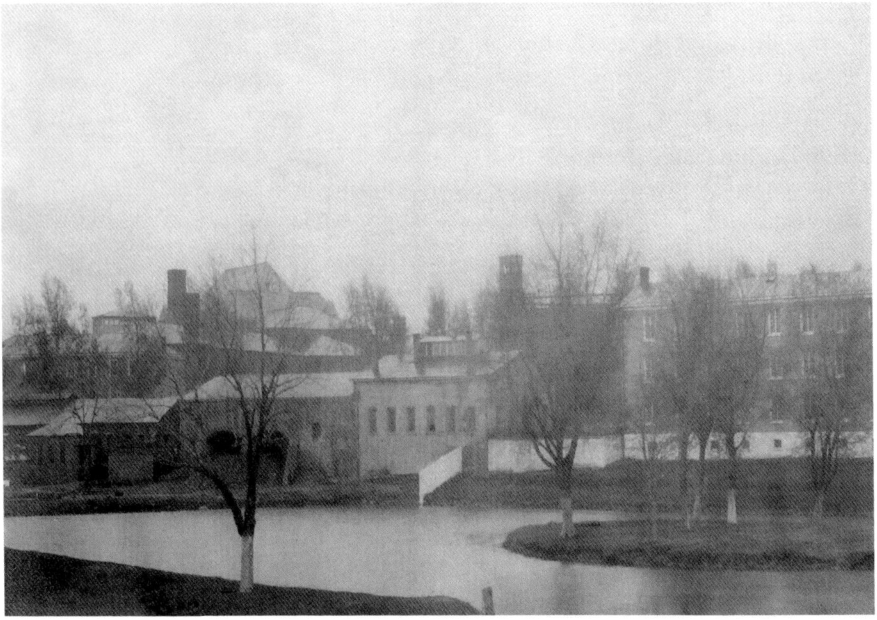

The house of correction in Holmesburg was always used for balloon flights since it housed the gasworks for the community. Gas was need for flight since it was used to inflate the balloons of the day.

only a short trip in mind, Atherholt took off from Stuttgart, Germany, on October 27, 1913. He encountered winds and bad weather and could not land. He remained in the air until he got a break in the clouds one week later. Finally, setting down inside the Russian border, Atherholt landed in the middle of a military encampment of Russian soldiers. Initially, he was accused of being a German spy. Questioned and held for days, he suffered from extreme exposure and food deprivation. After intensive interrogation by the Russians, Atherholt was released and he returned to America.

Although there is no evidence that Atherholt was welcomed by parades or celebrations, he became one of Holmesburg's most recognized and admired citizens. He quietly returned to his wife, Helen Middleton, and two daughters, Roselyne and Elizabeth, and lived the next year and a half in his home at 8006 Frankford Avenue. He died suddenly of a heart attack in his forty-eighth year at his home on April 15, 1915. At his funeral services, he was remembered as Philadelphia's "most noted aeronaut." His grave site can be found in the Emmanuel Episcopal Church Cemetery of Holmesburg.

Holmesburg Improvement Association 1909–1914

One of the recent additions to the Historical Society of Frankford's Center for Northeast History is the minute book of the Holmesburg Improvement Association for the years 1909–14. Improvement associations were common in Northeast Philadelphia in the late nineteenth and early twentieth centuries. Composed of men who were prominent citizens in the community, these associations took upon themselves the responsibility of supervising many of the tasks that now are done by the City of Philadelphia. The need for such associations was caused by the lack of concern by the city for the many small villages in the Northeast sections of Philadelphia. In 1910, the paid staff for Holmesburg consisted of eight workers, seven federal and one city. With such a small workforce, it fell to these improvement associations to run the villages.

Meeting once a month at Athenaeum Hall, the Holmesburg Improvement Association received reports about the condition of the town. Officials were elected and committees formed to deal with various issues of the day. Notes found in the Holmesburg minute book give an example of how associations

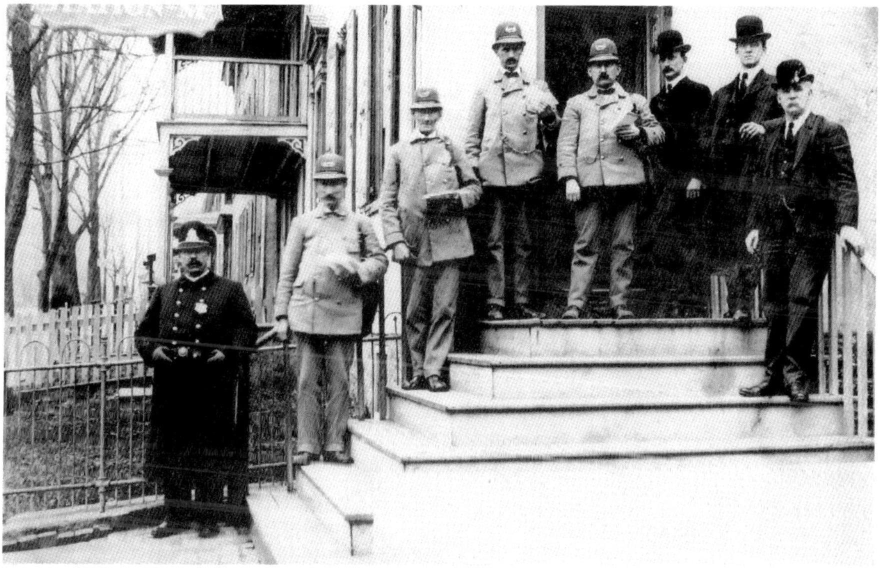

An 1880 picture of Holmesburg's paid village officials. There were four postmen, one policeman, two post office clerks and one supervisor. Here they are pictured in front of the post office at Frankford Avenue and Welsh Road. Without paid city officials, responsibility for getting things done in Holmesburg fell to the Holmesburg Improvement Association.

were organized and how they effected change in their community. Specific to Holmesburg in 1909–14 were the following issues: transportation, cleanliness, safety, new technologies and monitoring the Philadelphia city budget.

Transportation issues in the Northeast in 1910 centered on getting cheaper transportation into the city. The main complaint was the ten-cent fare. People living in Holmesburg paid five cents to get to Frankford and then five cents to ride to center city. Holmesburg residents demanded a five-cent fare to center city. The association wrote and met with local trolley companies but failed to get the policy changed until the 1920s.

Another issue was the cleaning of streets where trolley tracks ran. There was an amendment to trolley line contracts that stated that the company would clean the streets. For Holmesburg that meant that Frankford Avenue should have been cleaned by the trolley company. This was seldom done. Appeal after appeal by the association did little to spur action from the trolley company, which might have sent a crew of men once or twice a year. The association appealed to William Patterson, superintendent of the house of correction, for prison gangs to be sent to clean the streets and lots of Holmesburg. So it was that Holmesburg got its streets cleaned and snow removed by prisoners from the house of correction. Prisoners "volunteered" to do the work and were accompanied by a guard. The cost to the improvement association was the same for each project—$4.50 for tobacco for the prisoners.

One issue that plagued the association for years was that the requests from those who lived near State Road and Rhawn Street called for an extension of Rhawn Street to the Delaware River. This would have provided all of Holmesburg with a direct commercial route to the sea. Local residents and those of the Birkmann Hotel at Rhawn and State Road would profit greatly from such a river route. The issue was decided when they transferred the Blockley poorhouse to that river site, thus blocking a possible extension. Residents then asked the association to petition Philadelphia mayor Rudolph Blankenburg for an extension of the Torresdale Avenue trolley line from Cottman to Blakiston Street. The mayor rejected the request, stating that there were no houses on Torresdale Avenue between Cottman Street and Rhawn Street, and only thirty-eight houses near Rhawn Street and Torresdale Avenue; therefore the trolley companies determined that it would not be a profitable investment. The association accepted this decision unhappily and again felt neglected by the city.

The second-highest number of complaints brought to the association centered on the cleanliness of the village. Without city services, the burden fell to the association, which solved the problem through community cooperation. Lots would be cleaned by owners, as was the case on August 8, 1913, when Maxwell Rowland removed "offensive" materials from his Craig Street lot. Citizens were encouraged to finish their street walks with bricks. The association could arrange the purchase of one thousand bricks for nine dollars. The association also arranged for the laying of bricks at Frankford Avenue and Rhawn Street, four blocks in all directions, to promote a mud-free environment. Finally, with the help of Superintendent William Patterson of the house of correction, a schedule was arranged to have periodic street cleaning by the prisoners and sprinkling to keep dust down in the summertime.

A third issue that fell to the association was the community's adjustment to new technology. In many ways, the village of Holmesburg in the early 1900s was the same town founded by the Holme and Crispin families two hundred years before. New utilities such as water and gas required the installation of water- and gas lines. Formerly, waterlines were found only on Rhawn Street, and Frankford Avenue water came from the Tacony-Holmesburg Waterworks Reservoir on Frankford Avenue across from the new Holme Library at Hartel Street. The gas came from the house of correction, but sometimes it was not clear-burning in light fixtures. Nevertheless, new gaslights were placed outside the churches and Athenaeum Hall on Frankford Avenue, the first streetlights on Holmesburg's main street. The association was given the task of issuing a complaint to the gas supplier, the house of correction. The gas issues went unresolved until the 1920s, when electricity was introduced in Holmesburg.

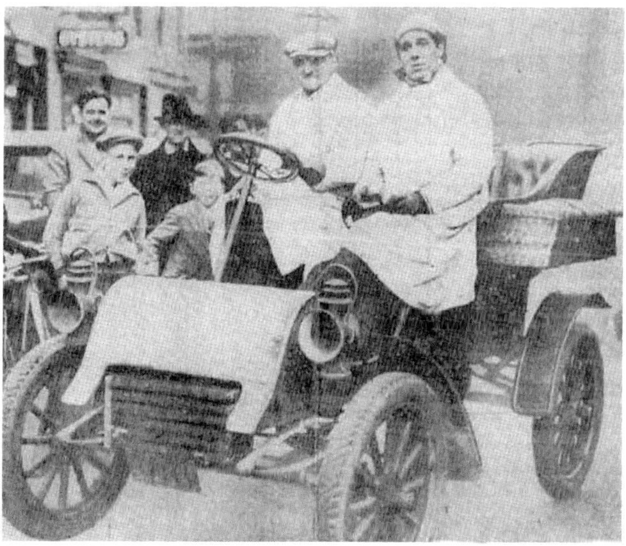

A picture taken in Holmesburg of a 1902 Tin Lizzie car. Horseless carriages brought many new problems to the village of Holmesburg. They sped through the village at thirty miles per hour, kicked up dust and frightened the horses. It was a continuous concern for the members of the local improvement association.

The biggest change in the community was the introduction of the automobile. Although there were only a handful of cars in the Northeast in the early 1900s, Frankford Avenue was a favorite spot to take a ride in the country. The committee was asked to do something about the speed of the cars, which often exceeded thirty miles per hour as they passed through Holmesburg. Horses became frightened and children in the streets were at risk. No solution was proposed, as this was a time when no stop signs or traffic lights existed.

An innovative proposal considered by the association was the building of playgrounds for children. The association appointed a committee, purchased playground equipment and built the Brown and Crispin playgrounds. The association even built a playroom for the girls of the community on the third floor of the Brown School. When a request to the city for gas lighting was refused, the association bought the supplies and the lighting fixtures and had gas piping installed.

One technique used by the city to save money was to allocate funds for projects and then not spend the money. Such an incident was recorded on June 13, 1913, when it was reported that $69,000 that had been appropriated for Pennypack Park remained unspent. The association sent a representative to the City Park Commission to demand an explanation. No response is found in the minutes to indicate that the issue was ever settled. It is clear from these early years that negotiations between Holmesburg and the City of Philadelphia usually left Northeast Philadelphia residents distrustful of city officials.

The minutes of the Holmesburg Improvement Association 1909–14 can be found in the Center for Northeast History Collection at the Frankford Historical Society.

FORREST HOME REMEMBRANCES, 1916–1923

These remembrances were written by eighty-five-year-old Grace Gross about her six-year stay at the Forrest Home for Aged Actors in Holmesburg from 1916 to 1923. Her father was the caretaker and gardener for the property. Grace went to the Forrest Home with her father when she was two years old just after her mother died. Recapture the beauty and simplicity of these earlier days as told by Grace Gross.

The Forrest Home grounds began near Cottman Avenue, went north on Frankford Avenue, almost to present day Sheffield Street, and then east on Sheffield Street to Torresdale Avenue. The front of the home faced the Delaware River, which you could see from the upstairs veranda.

The grounds were beautiful; fruit trees, little streams about, with watercress growing. Formal paths all led into a huge circle. Roses, raspberries, gooseberries, and almost any flower you could name bloomed there. Also a vegetable garden and grape arbors with large branches filled with grapes located in the rear near Frankford Avenue.

All the actors and actresses were my friends. I walked with them and talked with them and shared the beauty of the home. I was allowed to go into the home anytime I wished. I especially enjoyed the library and of course the kitchen, where Emma the cook ruled. [Emma was an African American whose family lived in Holmesburg.] In the library stood the knight in armor guarding the 6,000 books, the small bronze bust and marble statue of Edwin Forrest caste in a Shakespearian character done by an artist of a bygone day.

In the next room, I can see the beautiful dining room where all the residents eat their meals: the ladies in silks and laces; the gentleman in dark impressive suits with stiff collars and flowing ties. The furniture is impressive, too. Mahogany sideboards with large fruits carved by the hand of a skilled craftsman and serving tables and tea carts with silver pots and sparkling glasses.

I can see Emma in the kitchen busy as ever. Later, I will go around to the kitchen door, give a little tap, and Emma will say, "Come in little girl."

Delicious smells are the fascination of this kitchen. Many a corn muffin and large round cookies with icing I have had there. Then with a tall glass of lemonade and a pat Emma would send me on my way, down the tan gravel path where Daddy was working under the Ginko tree. The leaves were like little fans. We go down the path to the carriage house. I enter the dark building to see the black shiny carriage that awaits it's Sunday trip to take the actors and actresses to St. Dominic's Church on Frankford Avenue. Emmet, my Dad's helper, will don his high black hat and black coat for the trip. Then he will get Ned the horse into his harness, drive around to the back entrance of the home and pick-up his passengers in all their Sunday finery.

Then my thoughts fly back to the time Houdini visited the home. I was so excited to see his entourage enter the driveway between the huge brownstone pillars. The iron gates were already open for him. Houdini had a car not a carriage. He was all dressed in black, black cap and hat with a wide brim. I will always remember that day.

Each year on Edwin Forrest's birthday, there was an elaborate party. Guests and sponsors all came in carriages and chauffeur-driven cars. The party was held on the front lawn of the home facing the Delaware. They had all sorts of entertainment. I was happy and delighted to be a part of it. My

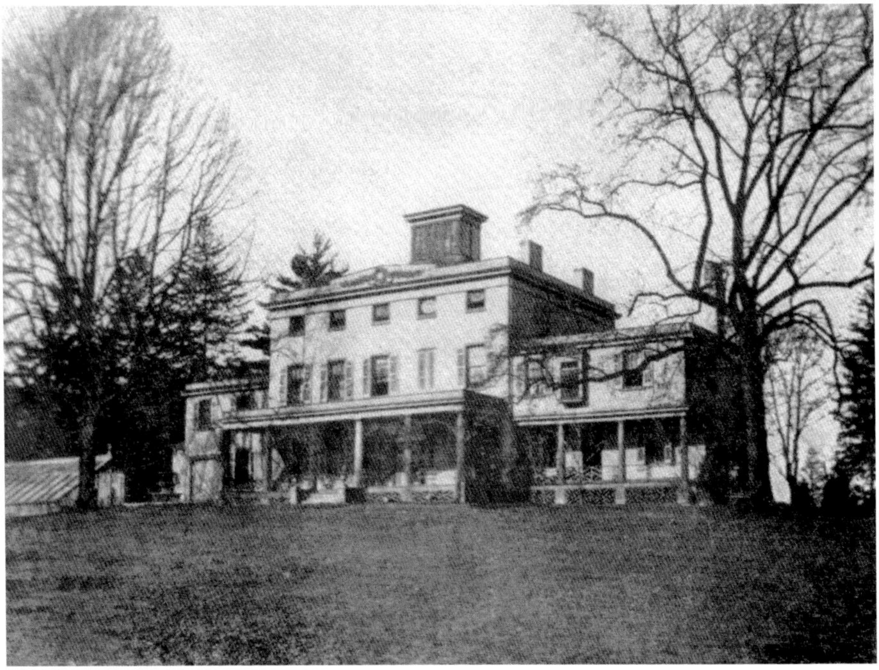

The front lawn of the Edwin Forrest Home, facing the Delaware River. This large lawn was used for parties and celebrations. The garden's hothouse is on the left (1920).

best friends from the home were there: Amy Lee, Percy Plunket and Mrs. Stone, they cheered me on. They were my dearest friends at the home.

Amy Lee gave me lovely things. She had trunks of old stage costumes in the storeroom. She gave me purple shoes and purple silk stockings, old purses and costume jewelry, trinkets and pink skirts.

Mrs. Stone was blind and a sweet, dear lady. I always took her to the garden to smell the sweet briar roses. Mrs. Stone's room smelled of camphor balls. She would open her drawer and give me little bits of candy. I used to tell her I liked them, but then I'd slip them in my pocket.

I did naughty things once in a while. The roses would just be showing a little color and I would peel the green part off so it would be pink. I forgot to tell you Amy Lee used to eat the gooseberries in the garden and horrors of all horrors expectorate the skins on Dad's perfect paths. It was a beautiful formal garden, and everything had to be perfect. When I rode my tricycle, I would not dare to go on the perfect edges.

Percy Plunket used to sit on one of the benches at the lower gate where I would visit him. He always was dressed formally. His snow white hairs flowing and looked truly like a Shakespearean actor that he was. By his bench in the woods behind the front gate stood a field of white violets. A little back in the woods was a grave where one of the actors was buried. It was his wish that he be buried there. Each spring I would gather a bunch of the white violets and some May apple blossoms and place them on his grave. No one ever seemed to bother and I thought he might like it. Later I was told that he had been on stage when Abraham Lincoln was shot at Ford's Theatre.

It was getting late and time to go to the gardener's cottage, located on the grounds of the home. It's a lovely house, with cozy rooms and windows with diamond shaped panes. The big black stove in the kitchen welcomes us. It is large, shiny and polished everyday. At night my father and I sit around the kitchen table, I with my homework from J.H. Brown School and my Dad with his seed catalogs. We see by a large oil lamp which has always been in use at our home. No electricity but as some people in Holmesburg are proving, it will come.

My dad and I talk a little. We reminisce about the time the Gypsies came down Frankford Avenue and into our orchard and thought they'd found a lovely place for their wagons. Dad of course went immediately and told them they could not stay. He did allow them to stay the night and also to gather some fruit. They were fascinating with their bright and colorful clothes and their long, dangling earrings. They looked like bright gold to me, but probably were not.

When I was seven years old, we left the Forrest Home. The residents were moved into the old Castor mansion on Solly Avenue where Grover Cleveland was once entertained. Within the year they were relocated to their new Edwin Forrest Home at 1845 Parkside Avenue in Overbrook.

The builders and developers who purchased the Forrest Home for Actors Estate for $600,000 established the streets too close together and made them too small for the number of row homes they were building. It was sheer greed that made the section the way it is today.

FORREST HOME HISTORY, 1876–1927

For those who study history, few events are as simple as they first appear. The Forrest Home for Aged Actors in Holmesburg is an example of this phenomenon. The story of the home's founding and fifty years of existence seems at first to be nothing more than a magnanimous bequest by Edwin Forrest (1806–1872), America's most famous Shakespearean actor in the nineteenth century, to establish a home for retired actors. His bequest provided security and comfort for retired actors and also helped to bestow upon the little village of Holmesburg a culture and civility that had not existed in Northeast Philadelphia before.

Edwin Forrest purchased the home known as Springbrook in 1865 from George H. Stuart for $94,000 at a public auction with lawyer John McCullough bidding for him. It was strictly an investment. Forrest, who had a mansion on North Broad Street (now the Freedom Theatre), had little desire to live at Springbrook. The Edwin Forrest Home (1876–1927), as Springbrook came to be known, was located west of Frankford Avenue between present-day Sheffield and Teesdale Streets east to Torresdale Avenue. It contained six bedrooms, a large dining area, a massive library of six thousand books and a large parlor for entertaining visitors. Placing two people in each bedroom gave the home a maximum capacity of twelve retired actors at a time. The mansion contained many stage artifacts and works of art, the most spectacular being a large statue of Edwin Forrest as Coriolanus in Shakespearean garb. There were pictures gracing the walls in every room in the house, including the famous gallery of Matthew Brady photos of Forrest as Spartacus and the Indian prince Metamora. Even today, these photos are considered among Brady's best work. No one who entered could deny the culture, grace and beauty of the home.

Edwin Forrest was one of the most controversial figures of his day. He helped to spark the Astor Place nativist riot in 1849 when his animosity toward English actor William Macready precipitated a fight that left twenty-two people dead in the streets of New York. Later, in 1853, his very public divorce from his wife Catherine Sinclair allowed the world to learn of his infidelities and cruelties toward his wife. This alienated him from most of upper-class society in Philadelphia. The negative publicity and his audacity in never admitting that he did anything wrong only strengthened Forrest's appeal as an actor. He continued to draw large audiences to his performances, making him one of the city's richest men.

All of this was known to the people of Holmesburg when Forrest purchased Springbrook in 1865. But it wasn't until 1866 that ownership of the home became an issue in the village. In April 1865, the assassination of Abraham Lincoln by actor John Wilkes Booth changed the attitudes of Americans toward the theatre. Actors began to be held in low regard, if not disdain, throughout the country. Forrest himself was implicated by association with Booth since Booth's older brother Edwin was named after Forrest. Forrest had a special bond with actors and tried to support them as best he could. Secretly, he saw to it that actors who could not get work because of their Southern sympathies or allegiance to Booth had a place to live. He opened his newly acquired home in Holmesburg to his actor friends who had been blackballed from the stage. Seeing how it helped them, he summoned his lawyer and wrote his will in 1866, establishing upon his death a home at Springbrook for aged actors and actresses. For the next five years, actors and actresses continued to come and go at Springbrook as their fortunes on stage became untenable. To many in Holmesburg, Springbrook had become a place that lacked respectability, and Forrest seemed unwilling to do anything about it.

About the same time, Holmesburg had become home to about a dozen former Union Civil War officers. Men like community leaders John Holme, Lewis Pattison and Kelby Smith, all returning Union officers, expressed concern about who was living in the Forrest house. The Forrest house had become a controversial issue in the village. Rumors circulated daily as to who had moved in and what their loyalties were.

Relief from the impasse came when Edwin Forrest died in December 1872, and his will revealed that Springbrook would become a home for aged actors. The Edwin Forrest Home officially opened in 1876, after years of litigation. A board of managers was elected, and entrance requirements were developed for those who wished to apply for admission to the home. Still,

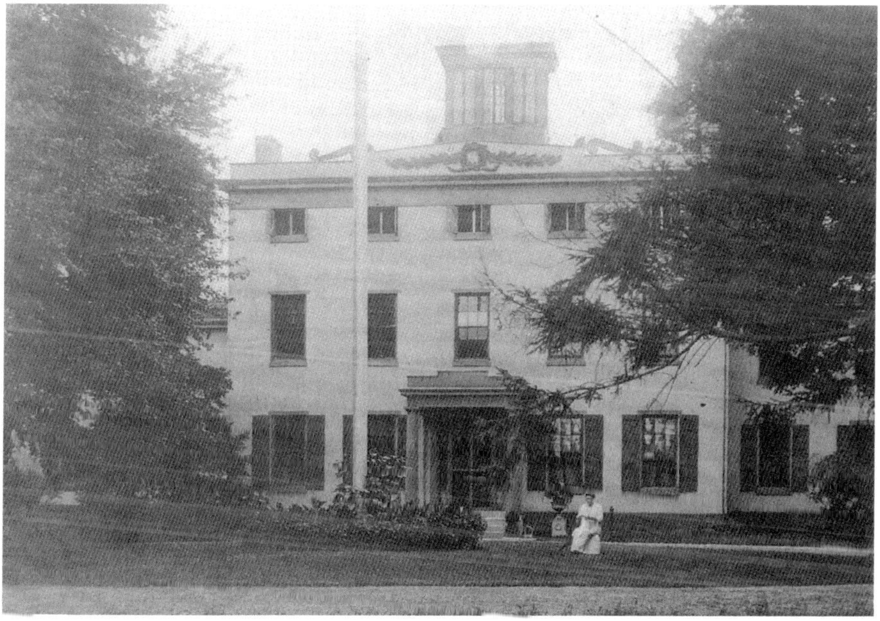

The rear of the Edwin Forrest Home that faced Frankford Avenue. This view was most common to Holmesburg residents.

community leaders of Holmesburg remained apprehensive about the newly organized home, since the proposed members of the board of managers were all from the theatre, longtime admirers of Edwin Forrest and outsiders to the village. Given these circumstances, Holmesburg citizens adopted a "wait and see" attitude about the newly formed organization.

Two major requirements for admission to the home were enacted by the board of managers. To prove their worthiness, all actors wishing to live there had to submit a portfolio of their work on stage (although those who had worked with Forrest gained great favor). Second, they had to agree that if they were accepted they would participate in three public events each year at the home. They were to read from the Declaration of Independence on July 4, perform Shakespeare on his birthday and discuss Forrest's greatest roles on *his* birthday. The patriotic reading each year on the Fourth of July did a great deal to ease tensions created between the home and the village.

While these developments created greater enthusiasm for the Forrest Home in Holmesburg, they did little to ease the belief that a board of managers located in center city was too far removed to know what was happening in the home. Was there not someone locally who could serve as superintendent of the Forrest Home for the board of managers? The opportunity presented itself when the position was created, and Austrian-born Andreas Hartel (Hartel Street was named in his honor)—who had just retired from owning and managing the Pennypack Calico Print Works in 1892—became available. Hartel had long been active in Holmesburg, serving on the board of the Lower Dublin Academy, as a vestryman of Emmanuel Church and as a leader in the Holmesburg Improvement Association, and he had been recently added to the board of managers of the Forrest Home. Everyone in Holmesburg was happy when Hartel applied for the position. He got it in 1893. He brought a whole new spirit to the home. He made it more a part of the village by holding its three main cultural events in different parts of the town and by having children and schools participate in larger numbers. Next, he encouraged two members from the Forrest Home to become active in the Holmesburg Improvement Association. Members of the home were now working for the improvement of the village. By the time of Andreas Hartel's death on May 3, 1911, he had created a new spirit of cooperation between Holmesburg citizens and the managers of the Forrest Home. Never again would there be a question about the loyalties of those who lived there. The home continued to operate in Holmesburg until 1927, when it moved to Overbrook. It closed in 1986, after merging with a similar home, the Lillian Booth Actor's Home in Englewood, New Jersey.

In the end, the Forrest Home for Actors provided the Holmesburg community with a cultural lifestyle nonexistent in Northeast Philadelphia communities north of Frankford. Holmesburg was, from the beginning, a highly diverse community that grew by emphasizing culture, history, civility and love of knowledge in its schools. No wonder that so many Holmesburg natives take such pride in their community and its history.

GREENBELT KNOLL: SUCCESSFUL RACIAL INTEGRATION, 1956–PRESENT

Greenbelt Knoll in Northeast Philadelphia was the first planned integrated development in Philadelphia and among the first in the nation. Developer Morris Milgram, a pioneer in the nation's open housing movement, began building Greenbelt Knoll in 1956 and placed in the deeds the requirement that 55 percent of the buyers must be white and 45 percent nonwhite. The people who moved there were "swimming against the tide in the 1950s," remarked Dr. Thomas Sugrue, a history professor at the University of Pennsylvania who is writing a book on civil rights in the North. "Their actions were as important as the freedom marchers in Mississippi."

Morris Milgram was the son of an Orthodox Jew who had fled religious persecution in Russia and settled in the Lower East Side of New York City. Educated in the public schools of New York, Morris went on to the City College of New York in 1933. He was asked to leave the college in 1934 after leading a campus protest against fascism. After graduating from Dana College (now a part of Rutgers University), Milgram worked as an organizer for the Workers' Defense League. As part of his job, he helped Southern sharecroppers. Eventually, Morris became secretary of the National League. In 1947, he accepted an offer from his father-in-law to work at a small construction company in Philadelphia. Milgram's goal was to initiate the building of racially integrated housing.

Creating an integrated housing development before the civil rights movement was not an easy task. Milgram encountered resistance from contractors, bankers and realtors, but he raised enough money to buy a nine-acre tract of land opposite the Thomas Holme grave marker on Holme Avenue in Pennypack Park. The location had an advantage to Milgram in that it would be built in the woods that extended out of Pennypack Park, a feature he maintained by building the houses around the trees and preserving the forestlike atmosphere. Unfortunately, the owners would have to continually contend with the deer from the park that came into their neighborhood.

The homes originally sold for $20,000 in 1956 and were considered rather expensive at the time. Buyers had to have money and had to value an interracial and environmental lifestyle. These requirements set the stage for the development of a neighborhood that was self-consciously involved in a political and social movement that was ahead of its time. The first homes on Longford Street sold quickly, and by 1958 all houses had been sold.

The homes on the Longford Street cul-de-sac were all similar in appearance. They were single, one-story, rectangular homes with flat roofs, broad windows, natural wood siding and tubular metal chimneys reaching high into the sky. Designed by the well-known architectural firm Montgomery & Bishop, with input from the famed architect Louis Kahn, the Greenbelt Knoll homes looked nothing like the stone twins or brick row homes that dominated the area in the 1950s.

Residents of Greenbelt Knoll celebrated the fiftieth anniversary of the community on their cherished Longford Street in April 2008. Former residents flew in from New Delhi, Florida and Indiana. Grilled burgers, renewed friendships and hugs filled the day, and the stories exchanged told of a time when this racial experiment began.

One of the original homeowners on Longford Street, Virginia Barlow remembered her husband Roosevelt choosing lot three from the blueprints because he said that we will "need a house with few steps when we get old." Roosevelt Barlow, who went on to become one of Philadelphia's first African American fire captains, passed away in August 2003. Not long after, Virginia moved to a senior citizens home. "But the neighbors in Greenbelt Knoll always took care of me," Barlow says. "They hated to see me move."

When Larry Schwartz was in the sixth grade, his family made a conscious choice to buy a house in Greenbelt Knoll. Now a spokesperson for the U.S. Embassy in New Delhi, India, Schwartz remembers that it "took incredible commitment to move into this community in the 60s," but it "taught me to live with people who are different."

Luminaries from all walks of life have called Greenbelt Knoll home. Robert Nix Sr., who in 1958 became the first African American from Pennsylvania to serve in Congress, was an original homeowner. So was the Reverend Leon Sullivan, founder of the Opportunities Industrialization Centers of America and a leading American civil rights leader. Pulitzer Prize–winning playwright Charles Fuller owns a home on Longford Street a short distance from wood furniture maker James Camp and his wife Cornella. Cornella recalls that they had not walked through the house yet but the rare chance to expand their children's horizons—to play alongside white children and frolic in the woods—was "the big draw." Builder Morris Milgram believed so much in his idea of a racially integrated community that he chose to live in the house on building lot five.

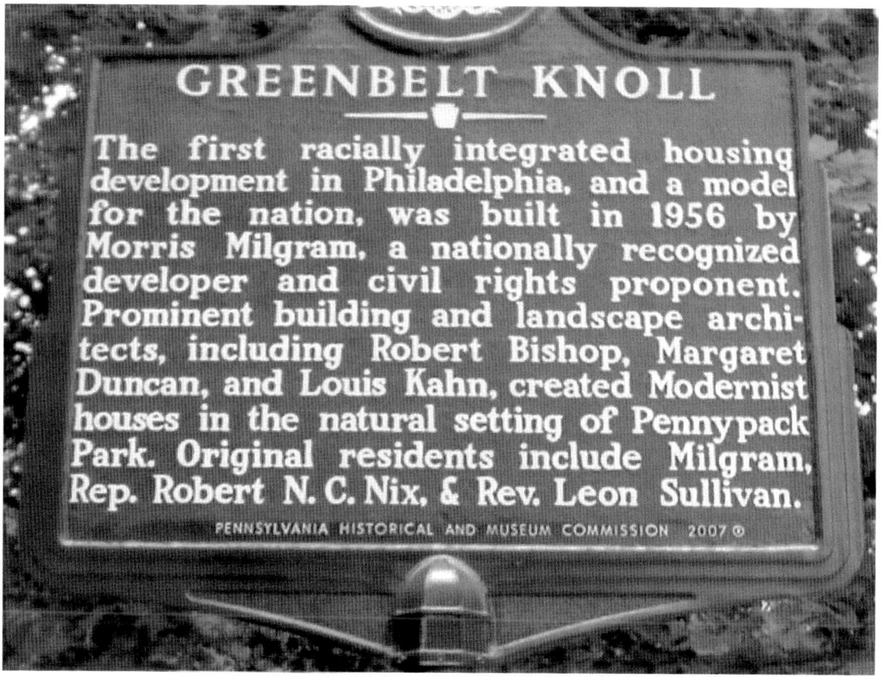

The Pennsylvania Historical and Museum Commission sign at the entrance of Longford Street near Holme Circle on Holme Avenue.

Morris Milgram died a decade ago, but Greenbelt Knoll remains even today a racially integrated community, retaining the original homes and their exteriors. It is one of Philadelphia's oldest and most successful racially utopian communities. A statement by Milgram in 1969 holds true today: "If we don't learn to live together, soon the world is going to come apart."

In March 2008, the Philadelphia Historical Commission designated Greenbelt Knoll a historic district, thereby helping to protect it against physical alterations and demolition that could destroy its architectural integrity. Residents are now working with the state to have Greenbelt Knoll placed on the National Register of Historic Places, an honor of which it is certainly worthy.

Part II

Tacony

How Tacony Stopped Hitler's War Machine in 1941

Few in Northeast Philadelphia can remember how involved Tacony was in supporting President Roosevelt's preparations for World War II. The story begins in 1939, when Germany overran Poland and England declared war on Germany. The United States stood by and watched as the war intensified.

France was overrun quickly by swift Panzer attacks. Russia and Germany surprised the world by signing a peace agreement, leaving England alone to fight Germany. Germany would break the pact by invading Russia at the end of July 1941. Roosevelt stood strongly behind England. In May and June of 1941, the United States publicly began debating how to react to the conflict. Charles Lindbergh advocated support for Germany; Ambassador to Great Britain Joseph Kennedy implored Roosevelt not to fully support England because he felt they were losing the war. A peace movement began forming across the country based on long-held beliefs that favored neutrality. Despite these sentiments, Roosevelt decided to initiate a military buildup starting with the large industrial centers of the nation. It was then that the United States Department of Defense offered to finance building an armor plate factory at Disston Saw Company in Tacony.

Given the antiwar sentiment in the country, why was Tacony chosen as one of the early sites for a prewar military buildup? For those who knew Tacony, the decision seemed logical. Tacony had always been pro–Great Britain since its founding by Englishman Henry Disston in 1872. As early as 1879, British values and culture dominated in Tacony, a community that

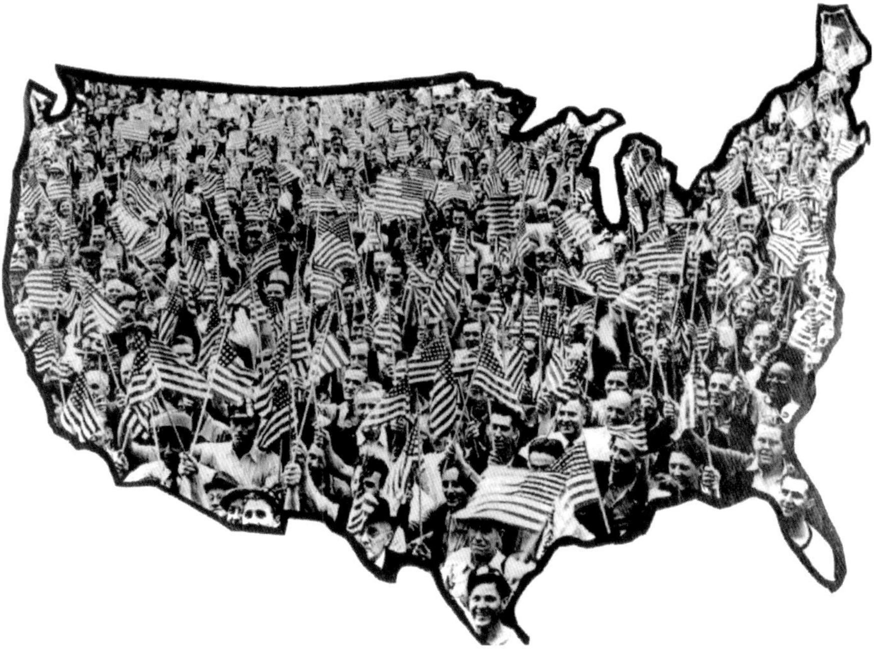

Crowd of Disston workers celebrating the building of the power plant and the armor plate facility in 1940. This picture was used throughout the country to show that American workers supported the buildup for war.

featured teahouses and English football (soccer) games. In 1884, English culture became even more imbedded in Tacony when two hundred steel smelters and their families were recruited from Sheffield, England, to work at the Disston Saw Company.

Another event favorable to the site choice was that Disston Saw had a reputation dating back to the Civil War of switching production schedules away from saws to producing what the government considered war necessities. During the Civil War, the firm produced armor plate for the Union navy that was used on the sides of wooden ships blockading the ports of the South. (This made futile the efforts by the Confederates to sink Union ships with floating mines.) In World War I, the Disston Saw Company produced bulletproof steel plates used on cannons and tanks. In 1941, the community showed its full support for Great Britain. A rally that featured the waving of British flags was held at Disston Playground. Over two thousand people gathered to hear speakers and local leaders decry Germany's bombing of London. With this background, government officials felt that Tacony stood ready to help Roosevelt's campaign to help England.

The federal government approved payment for two new facilities at Disston's Longshore and State Road plant. First, a power plant was designed to increase power throughout the plant in order to operate new wartime machinery. This upgrade would be put to good use if war came. Second, a new armor plate building was built to provide space for the production of bulletproof steel for tanks, cannons, halftracks and lightweight seats to protect pilots from air attacks from the rear.

A rally was organized in October 1942 by the Disston Company to open and dedicate the armor plate building officially and to lay the cornerstone for the power building. Famous radio personality Lowell Thomas served as master of ceremonies, and radio star Margaret Speaks was asked to sing "The Star-Spangled Banner." Acting Philadelphia mayor Bernard Samuels, federal government officials, union chiefs and Disston management were featured as speakers. All 3,400 workers from the factory were given the day off and attended the event. Reporters streamed in from throughout the country to cover the story for national publications. The pictures and stories from that day became the rallying cry for the nation for support of the war.

Pictures of Disston workers waving American flags at the event were featured in *Life* magazine on July 7, 1941. In magazines and newspapers around the world, a lengthy article entitled "Arming of America" featured the Tacony story. The picture of flag-waving workers from Disston Saw was placed inside a map of the United States and became a classic war image. Such pictures were used to show that Americans supported the war effort and were gearing up to help England and France. Journalists remarked on the patriotism of Disston workers. "In sharp contrast to recent pictures of striking defense workers waving demand-banners for more pay is this photo of flag waving workers, taken at the recent dedication of a new armor plate plant in Tacony, Pennsylvania. They are employees of Henry Disston and Sons, which expects the new plant to triple the firm's capacity for making armored plate for warships and other military uses."

Nevertheless, there were doubters of this support for war by the Tacony community. S. Horace Disston, president of the company, received many negative reactions. A mill-supply buyer at the Hart Heavy Hardware Company warned that the change to war production was not conducive to producing non-war products. "We hope that this means that you will be able to take care of your jobbers in a much better manner than you have in the past. We realize that national defense comes first but we believe also that your old customers should be given a certain amount of consideration also."

S. Horace Disston also received compliments for "standing tall" in a time of national crisis: "So many factories have seemed to be holding back; but

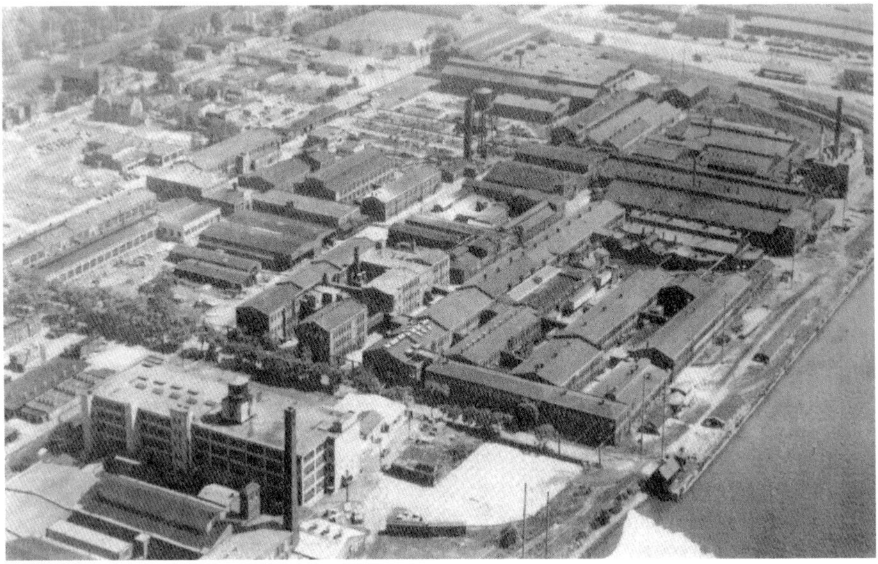

Henry Disston's factory complex in 1942. Tacony was originally a one-factory town with most workers relying on Disston for work.

we are 100% for bringing this war to a successful conclusion as soon as possible and think it's just as much our war as it is anybody else's," he said. Even more encouraging was a note from businessman H.P. Aikerman, who wrote, "I have tacked the picture of your Disston workers on the wall behind my desk to remind me of what patriotism really is."

To the citizens of Tacony none of this mattered. Their little town was now featured in *Life* magazine, movie houses, newspapers and national victory posters produced by the government. Tacony had become a national symbol of patriotism and loyalty for the country. It was a special place to live during World War II.

All quotations are taken from Harry C. Silcox, A Place to Live and Work, *pp. 133–37.*

THE TACONY-PALMYRA FERRY, 1922–1929

As the number of people and cars in Northeast Philadelphia increased in the 1920s, there was need for better access to New Jersey and the shore points. Prior to 1922, you would have to travel to the Market Street Ferry in downtown Philadelphia if you wished to drive a car to New Jersey. You could also get to Atlantic City by train from center city.

It became obvious that a profit could be made from a ferry line to New Jersey from Northeast Philadelphia, but where would it be located? While Frankford was the largest community in the Northeast, it was financially prohibitive to build a ferry at Frankford's port at the foot of Bridge Street in Bridesburg. Cars to the ferry would overcrowd the streets, and it would be too expensive to enlarge streets and improve access to the ferry in these already developed areas.

The leader of the group of investors wishing to establish the ferry line was Charles A. Wright of Riverton, New Jersey. He was an influential businessman who had long dreamed of a direct connection to Pennsylvania. Wright formed the Tacony-Palmyra Ferry Company in 1922 and was elected its president. He and Edward G. Borer negotiated the New Jersey side of the ferry, while a group of men headed by Thomas South and Peter Costello handled issues on the Pennsylvania side. To them, the southern edge of Tacony at Levick Street seemed like the best site on the Pennsylvania side. Located in a thinly populated area between Tacony and Wissinoming, it had one great advantage: the nearby trolley barn and key transportation hub for the Holmesburg, Tacony and Frankford Trolley Company at State Road and Levick Street not far from the Delaware River. Trolleys ran continuously from 6:00 a.m. until midnight from Holmesburg or Frankford to the Tacony barn on Levick Street.

From 1900 to the 1920s, the Hop, Toad and Frog Line, as the trolley was called, was the most important line for the working public in the Northeast. With numerous companies located along State Road—firms like Dodge Steel, Disston Saw, American Glass Works and Eben-Hardin Textile Mill—for five cents the line provided for a cheap way to get to work for workers from Frankford, Bridesburg, Holmesburg and Tacony. The Eben-Harding Textile Mill was said to have a 75 percent Polish female workforce that lived in Bridesburg. They got on the trolley at Bridge Street and State Road to get to Tacony.

The Hop, Toad and Frog line was the classic Toonerville trolley line. With open cars covered by canvas in the winter, with outside rear platforms and no heat, it was not the most luxurious of rides. The cars would become overcrowded at peak travel times and often required passengers to disembark at the Levick Street hill to push the trolley up the hill to Magee Street. The line remained the major connection to the factories of Northeast Philadelphia until the late 1920s. The old car barn for the trolley is still standing today and is now the Insinger building just south of the Tacony-Palmyra Bridge.

The Levick Street location for the proposed ferry was ideal. The trolley provided transportation to the ferry for the major population centers of the

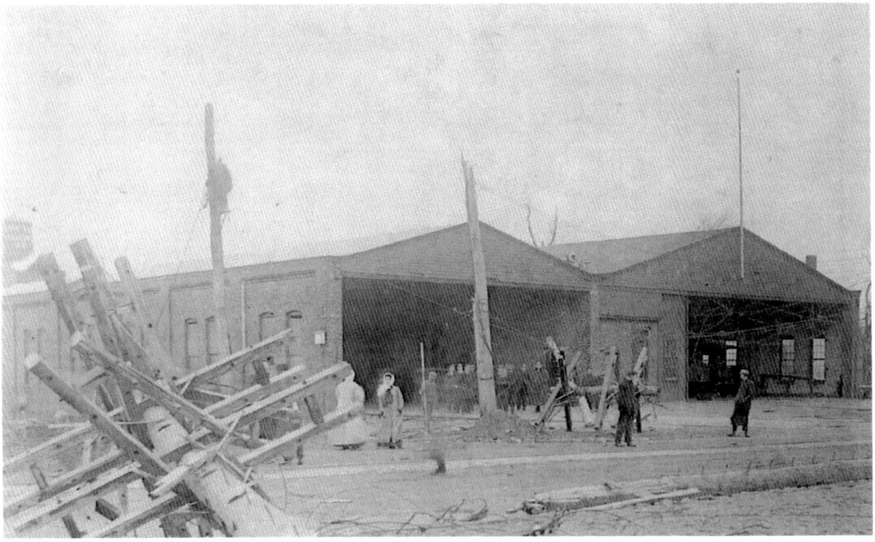

The car barn of the Hop, Toad and Frog Line that was located on State Road near the Levick Street entrance to the Tacony Ferry. The line ran from Frankford Avenue in Holmesburg east on Rhawn Street, south on State Road to Bridge Street and west on Bridge Street to Frankford Avenue. This was the best route on foot to the ferry.

Northeast, and there was enough open land and opportunities to improve automobile routes to the location without causing traffic congestion. The private investment group bought up land cheaply, installed Ferry Docks on both sides of the river, purchased two used ferryboats and began organizing the company in early 1922. Advertisements for the new ferry began to appear in newspapers noting that there would be no congestion or traffic jams for this "new route to the seashore."

Originally, the line was to operate between Tacony in Pennsylvania and Riverton in New Jersey, but protests by Riverton residents worried about traffic congestion forced a change to the New Jersey site. A new location several miles away in Palmyra at the foot of Cinnaminson Avenue was chosen. At 4:00 p.m. on May 6, 1922, the Tacony-Palmyra Ferry Company opened for business. Two ferries, the *Tacony* and the *Palmyra*, left from the foot of Levick Street from 6:00 a.m. until midnight seven days a week, sailing the 4,800-foot distance in fifteen minutes. The *Tacony* had been purchased from the Gloucester Ferry Company, while the *Palmyra* had been purchased from the Reading Railroad Company. The cost of the ferry was five cents for individuals and forty-five cents for cars and trucks. The *Palmyra* could carry eighteen cars and several hundred passengers, while the *Tacony* was a doubled-decker vessel that accommodated thirty-six cars and approximately five hundred passengers. A 1,100-foot-long driveway at the foot of Levick Street provided parking space for those waiting for the ferry.

In 1925, the ferries carried 410,567 cars, 115,890 foot passengers and 526,462 bus passengers. The success of the line prompted the City of Philadelphia to pave Frankford Avenue north of Longshore Street to Cottman Avenue and to pave Cottman Avenue to the Montgomery County Line to provide for east to west traffic to the ferry.

In addition to traffic and transportation to Tacony, there were larger social changes. The ferry site at the end of Levick Street became the location for numerous vendors selling New Jersey farm produce. It was not long before the Jersey tomato—cheap, tasty and readily available—became the rage of the community. One only has to read the *Disston Bits*, the Disston Company's weekly newsletter, to appreciate the popularity of the vendors. In fact, the markets and vendors along State Road were so popular that many housewives traveled from Holmesburg and Frankford to get fresh produce. At the end of each workday, the vendors would migrate to the company gates of Disston Saw, Dodge Steel and the Ebin-Harding Textile Mill to sell their goods. Workmen were often asked by their wives to shop for New Jersey produce or for candy and toys for the children.

From 1922 to 1929, the ferry promoted these new shopping and social patterns for the community. The ferry also established the future site of the bridge for Northeast Philadelphia. Heavy traffic on the ferries and an increased opportunity for profit prompted Charles A. Wright and Edward G. Borer to form the Tacony-Palmyra Bridge Company in 1927. When the bridge was opened on August 14, 1929, the ferry line closed for good. Forty-two of the ferry employees were hired by the new bridge company, while the remaining twelve found work at the Chester-Bridgeport Ferry Company. The community was especially pleased when the price of a trip to New Jersey was reduced to thirty-five cents. The opening of the bridge, along with the Frankford El and Roosevelt Boulevard in the same period, was a major impetus to the development of the Northeast.

THE TACONY-PALMYRA BRIDGE, 1929–PRESENT

The Tacony-Palmyra Ferry was so successful that by 1925 the board of directors could predict that a bridge over the same location could easily carry the projected break-even point of a million and a half cars each year. They pushed the New Jersey legislature to pass a law in 1925 that provided for the construction of additional bridges over the Delaware River. This followed construction of the Delaware River Bridge (known today as the Ben Franklin Bridge), which was started in 1924 and completed in 1926. It was then that the president of the Tacony-Palmyra Ferry, Charles L. Wright, and Riverton businessman Edward G. Bore organized the Tacony-Palmyra Bridge Company.

The designers and builders of the Delaware River Bridge—Modjeski, Masters and Chase—were chosen to design the new Tacony-Palmyra Bridge. A congressional act approved its construction on January 25, 1927, with final approval secured by the War Department on the last day of the same year. State and municipal approvals soon followed, and on February 14, 1928, construction began on the bridge, whose budget was estimated at $4.7 million.

The project was not without controversy. It came to light that a second plan was being considered by the bridge company that included a $20 million proposal to build the bridge high enough to clear all marine traffic on the river. At the time, the public did not consider bridge openings much of a problem for those who would be using the bridge. Also, the higher span would mean years of delay, which was unacceptable to all. The ensuing political storm left the idea of a drawbridge at a cost of $4.7 million as the best construction plan. As a result, the company fired several members of the staff and dismissed the secretary-treasurer of the Burlington County Bridge Commission. A second political storm arose when it was discovered that W.G. Borer owned the land on both sides of the river where the bridge would touch the shore. He had purchased the land in 1926 based on inside information and sold it to the bridge company for a large profit

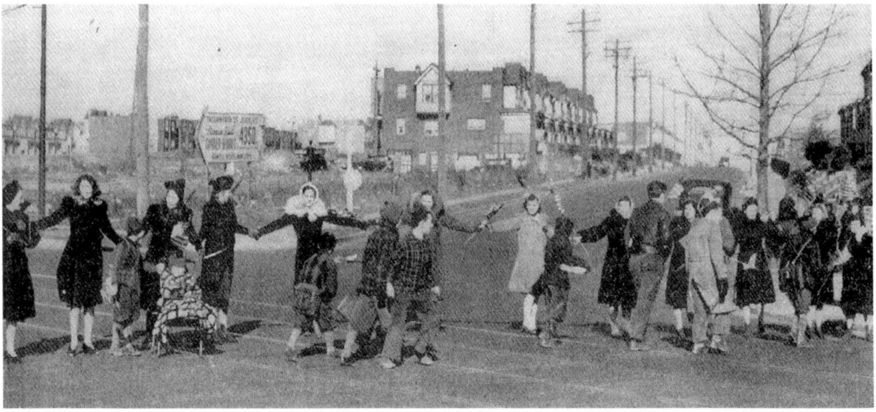

Parents of children from the Allen School protest the large volume of traffic going to the Tacony-Palmyra Bridge. A policeman was eventually assigned to the corner for traffic control. The protest took place in 1936 at Frankford Avenue and Levick Street.

on February 22, 1927. Today, such a practice could lead to a jail term, but because the bridge was being financed by private capital such activity was considered smart business practice and was unchallengeable by law. The savings to government for transportation costs paid by private business far outweighed concerns about questionable business practices.

Another concern of the community was the fact that four men were killed during bridge construction. Although most were not from Tacony, the bridge construction was dangerous work. Two men died falling from the steel girders and drowning in the Delaware River, a diver died in the decompression chamber after working at the bottom of the river on the foundation and another man died when one of the large stones used to construct the piers fell from a crane and killed him. Construction projects at that time were always dangerous, but to the people of Tacony this seemed excessive. Parents warned their children to stay away from the bridge site.

Despite all the controversies, construction continued on the bridge. The piers were set on March 27, 1918, and the main parts of the bridge were completed over the next year and a half. There were three main structures: the central arch in the center of the river, the 260-foot bascule span (a drawbridge-like section operated by counterweights to open the section to allow ships to pass) and three continuous spans, plus deck girder approaches via the viaduct spans. These were completed in the summer of 1929, and the bridge was set for its grand opening.

On that day, flags draped the bridge, patriotic music was played and speeches filled the air from 9:00 a.m. until the opening of the bridge at 3:00 p.m. Mayor Harry Mackey of Philadelphia told the crowd, "This bridge is one that fits into the coordinated plan of development of the great territory in this section on both sides of the river." Governor Morgan Larson of New Jersey predicted, "We have come here today to further transportation between two great states…Thus there will be a greater development of the two states joined." Ralph Modjeski, chief engineer for the bridge, stated optimistically that "this is a bridge with proper maintenance we hope will last 100 years."

The celebration on the opening of the bridge was one of the biggest events in Tacony's history. Cars lined up on the bridge early in the day. The bridge was free that day, and riders wished to have the honor and distinction of being the first across to New Jersey. The first motorist from Philadelphia was Edward M. Heenan of Robbins Avenue, while E.C. Cook of Kirkwood, New Jersey, was first from New Jersey. The first accident on the bridge happened an hour and a half after opening when Herbert Sparks of Olney was struck in the rear by John A. Kuhne of Oxford Street in Philadelphia.

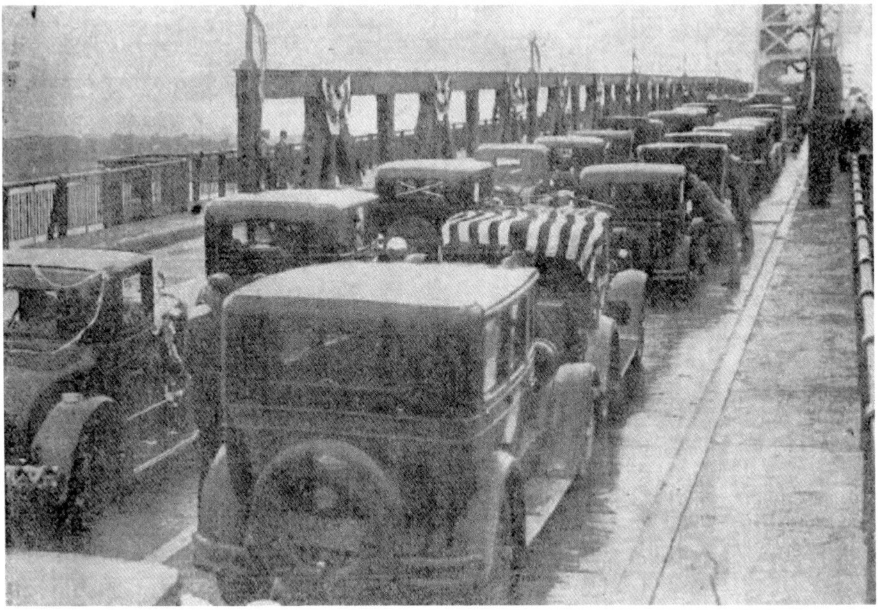

Cars line up on August 14, 1929, to be among the first to cross the Tacony-Palmyra Bridge.

The opening of the Tacony-Palmyra Bridge did not appear to play a significant role in the growth of Northeast Philadelphia. More important was the Frankford high-speed line. Most new building occurred at the time in the neighborhoods of Holmesburg, Mayfair and Oxford Circle. These areas were more dependent on the high-speed transportation provided by the Market-Frankford Elevated to get to work each day. As historian Sam Bass Warner has demonstrated, as systems of transportation developed in Philadelphia they depended on streetcars, roads and trains that led from the outskirts of the city into center city. From colonial days until today, workers have preferred to be within a half-hour of travel time to their jobs. The high-speed line to Frankford made the Northeast a half hour from center city.

What the bridge did reveal was a basic weakness in the road network in the city. There were few direct roads that crossed the city west to east in Northeast Philadelphia. Within months of the Tacony-Palmyra opening in 1929, over $18 million was budgeted for road projects in the area that fed into the bridge, including paving dirt roads and constructing access to the bridge. By 1931, over two million cars a year were using the bridge. While this made the bridge profitable, it also overcrowded the streets going to Tacony from Chestnut Hill, Germantown, Logan and Roxborough. Even though ample land and vacant ground existed that could have been purchased cheaply

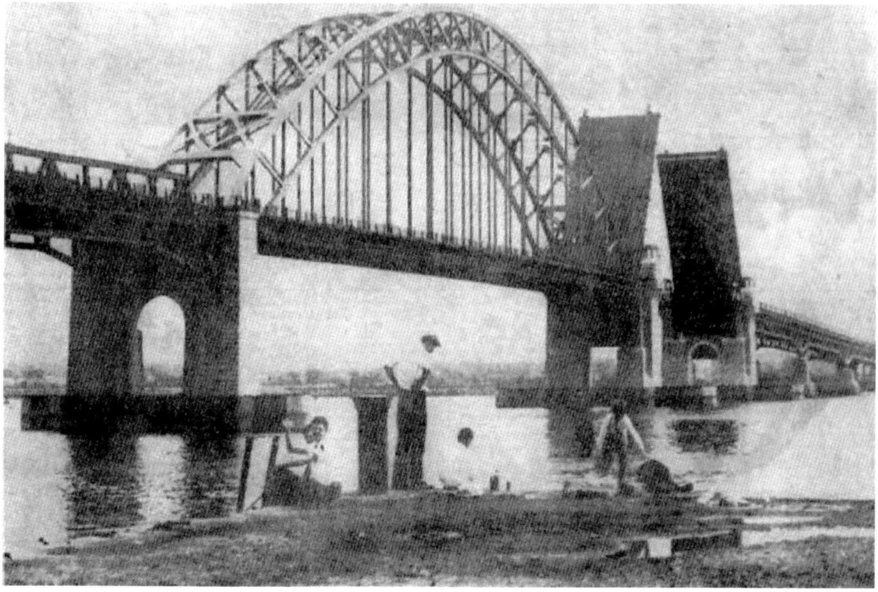

The Tacony-Palmyra Bridge on August 10, 1929. It was locked in the open position so that no one could cross the bridge prior to its dedication on August 14, 1929.

for a crosstown highway, the city did nothing. Local traffic was so bad in Tacony and Mayfair that protests were common, and maps were published every summer to show the best routes to the bridge. Officials from the city of Philadelphia complained about the millions of dollars needed to upgrade access streets to the bridge, money that was not in the city budget. The Great Depression quieted these complaints, as people had less money and there were fewer cars on the road, but it only delayed the problem of crosstown traffic for a later time. A 1971 plan to build the Pulaski Expressway west to east in Northeast Philadelphia became entangled in neighborhood disputes, and construction was never started. Today, only Woodhaven Road serves as a major west–east highway, and that is near the city's boundary, far from the bridge. Unfortunately, the post–World War II building explosion in Northeast Philadelphia overwhelmed the neighborhoods and allowed little space for crosstown highways. This remains to the present day the city's greatest neglect to the Northeast section of Philadelphia.

Despite these problems, the Tacony-Palmyra Bridge has proven to be a valuable asset to Northeast Philadelphia. It has given a higher profile to Tacony and provided easy access to New Jersey for Northeast Philadelphia residents and businesses. Modjeski's 1929 prediction of one hundred years of use for the bridge will undoubtedly become a reality.

ST. VINCENT'S HOME AND THE FOUNDING OF TACONY, 1859–PRESENT

A pivotal moment in Northeast Philadelphia history occurred on May 10, 1854, when Samuel Disston was reading the local ads in the newspaper. Samuel Disston was the brother of Henry Disston, owner of the Keystone Saw Works at Front and Laurel Streets in the Northern Liberties section of Philadelphia. Samuel's eye was drawn to an ad by St. Peter's German Catholic Church, which was selling vacation cottage lots to pay for a children's orphanage to be built on the Delaware River in the little village of Tacony in Northeast Philadelphia. The ad read:

> *A large piece of land was recently bought in Tacony with the intention that part of it be used for a German Orphan Asylum. The land is to be had for a cheap price of not more than $90 per building lot to be auctioned off on Tuesday May 13th at 11:00 o'clock…Ye all who pay rents in a silly corner of the city and breathe pestiferous air, soon losing dollars and life, come to Tacony! Start gardening and work that you won't get fat. You need not wrap sausages for the afternoon, lager beer waits for you on a ready table. And finally, honest people only invited for then Tacony will always be free of lawyers.*

Samuel Disston went to the auction and was satisfied with the validity of the offer. St. Peter's German Catholic Church, having need for a children's

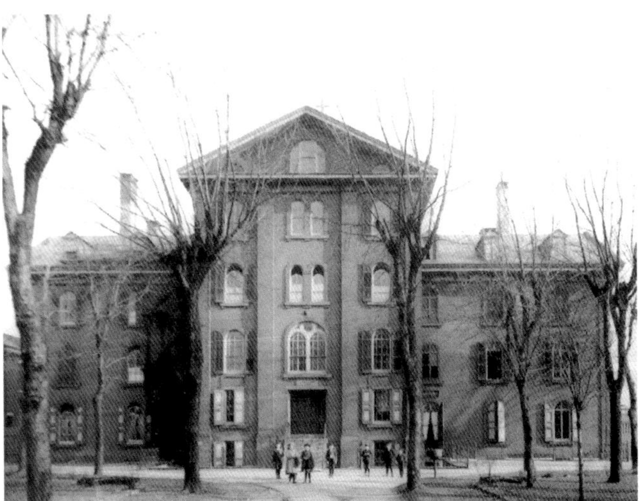

The St. Vincent Home, photo taken at the front gate entrance in Tacony in 1920. The home housed as many as four hundred orphans at a time.

orphanage, had formed the St. Vincent Cottage Association to arrange sales of the land. The association had purchased two farms comprising forty-nine acres on the Delaware near Tacony at a cost of $19,000. A portion of the land was set aside for the orphanage building, with the remainder being divided into vacation lots to be sold to raise the money necessary to build it. The price of a lot was $90, which was payable at a rate of $2 a month. Disston liked the terms of the offer and purchased a number of lots for the family.

Tacony at the time was a small village consisting of the Buttermilk Tavern, a railroad hotel and about a dozen houses. It was populated by boatmen and railroad men who lived by the Buttermilk Hotel dock and at the end of William H. Gatzmer's railroad line. Gatzmer had secured a charter for the Philadelphia and Trenton Railroad in 1846, but residents of Kensington refused to allow the railroad through their neighborhood, so the line terminated in Tacony. From there, travelers would get a boat to the city. The main economy of the town occurred in the summer months when farmers traveled from Bustleton and Holmesburg to stay at the Buttermilk Hotel and spend a few days fishing in the clear, clean waters of the Delaware River. There were boats to be rented and boys ready to help locate the best fishing spots. The vacation lots created even greater economic growth for the hotel, with over fifty city folk using its facilities.

Samuel Disston built his summer home in 1855 on what he described as one of the most beautiful and healthful spots along the Delaware. Easily accessible from the city, the Disstons could travel by steamboat to the Buttermilk Tavern dock and walk two hundred yards to their home. Henry Disston first saw Tacony when he vacationed with his brother in 1856.

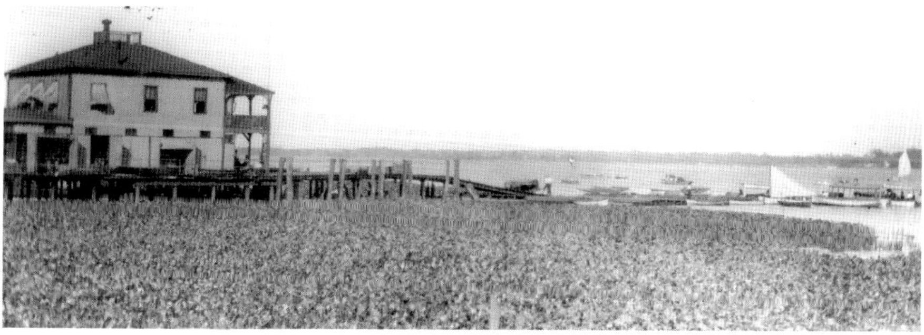

The Keystone Yacht Club on the Delaware River was built on land owned by St. Vincent and shared with the community. At one time this was an essential part of Tacony's river recreational activities.

Henry fell in love with the location and, during the Civil War, spent most of his summers there with his wife, four sons and daughter. The Disstons probably watched with interest the construction of the St. Vincent's Orphanage building in the 1850s and 1860s.

When the four-story St. Vincent's Home was completed in 1866, it was the largest structure in all of Northeast Philadelphia. With its entrance at the end of what became St. Vincent Street near Township Line Road (now Cottman Avenue), the home could be seen from Frankford Avenue. It was not very long before all of the farms along this stretch of Township Line Road were owned by German Catholics who worshiped at St. Vincent's Chapel every Sunday. The home had its own farm with chickens, pigs and cows. (All of this could be viewed by the residents of the Edwin Forrest Home for Aged Actors a few miles away in Holmesburg from the top of their house on Frankford Avenue.) The boys in the orphanage helped on the farm, while the girls made the uniforms worn by the children in the home. All prayed in German daily at the orphanage chapel. The home continued to grow in size so that by 1864, it housed 131 orphans of soldiers killed in the Civil War. Social and religious activities at St. Vincent's were an important part of Tacony's activities.

After the Civil War, Henry Disston was financially solvent because the factory had so many government war contracts. He did not like the factory's present location near Northern Liberties, however. He knew Tacony well and felt that it would be a good location to start his factory anew. There was great access to transportation on the river there, and rumors had it that

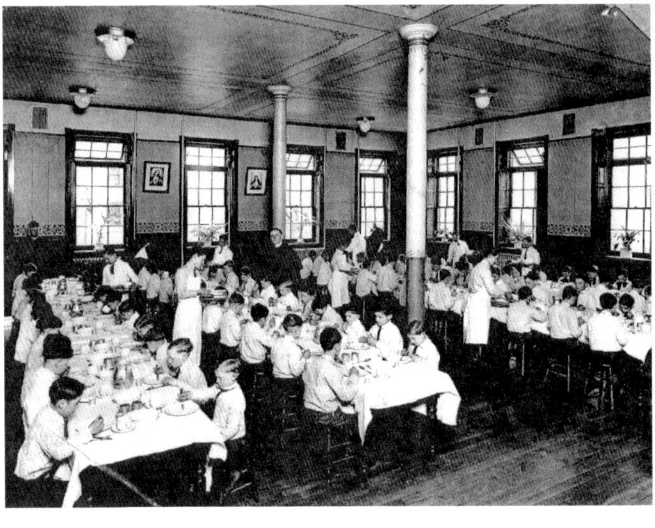

St. Vincent's boys' dining hall in the 1920s. The home was originally built for German-Catholic orphans but eventually was open to all.

the Tacony–Trenton railroad line would be purchased by the Pennsylvania Railroad and connected to the city by 1872. With all of this in mind, Henry Disston purchased the six-acre Buttermilk Hotel property and erected his first factory building, a saw handle shop, in 1872. He then began negotiations to buy all of the Tacony farms west of the railroad tracts to just east of Frankford Avenue. (He did not purchase the land on Frankford Avenue because it was too expensive at the time.) Disston had begun to fulfill his paternalistic vision of an ideal town by building a section of homes for his workers west of the railroad tracts. Tacony became the first utopian industrial town in a major city in America, rivaled only by railroad magnet George Pullman's town of Pullman in Chicago a few years later.

St. Vincent's remained an integral part of the new Tacony community. On Sundays its chapel served as the Catholic church for the region. Not only did many German Catholic farmers from the Cottman Street region come to St. Vincent's services, but other Catholic ethnic groups from Tacony also attended services there. This lasted until 1884, when the Irish Catholics of Tacony went to the Disston family and requested land for their own church. They explained that St. Vincent's was German and that they did not approve of their children learning their prayers in German. They wanted an Irish-Catholic church. Mary Disston, Henry's wife, gave them land at Unruh and Keystone Streets for a new church to be called St. Leo's. After years of effort, the German Catholics from St. Vincent's were able to build their own church

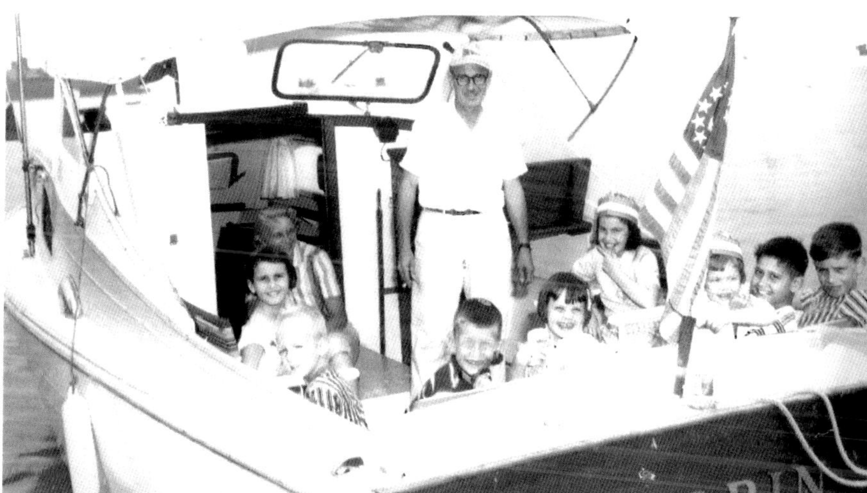

A member of the yachting club takes children from the St. Vincent Home for a ride on the Delaware River in the 1950s. Notice that few people wore life jackets on the river at that time.

at Torresdale Avenue and Cottman Street in 1913. The church lasted ten years, but the animosity shown toward Germans after World War I and low attendance forced its closing in 1923. The complex was then converted into St. Hubert's High School for Girls in 1924.

St. Vincent's grew into one of the largest and most successful orphanages in Philadelphia. The school at St. Vincent's served as the Catholic school of Tacony until 1906, when St. Leo's church opened its own school. World War I caused some disharmony in the home, however. St. Vincent's priests were German. Some of them were born in Germany and still had relatives there. They were very upset that their adopted country was at war with their homeland. Misunderstandings began to surface in Tacony over having German priests in the neighborhood. Still, the Tacony Keystone Yachting Club next door to St. Vincent's continued to give the children free boat rides, easing some of the controversy. After the war, St. Vincent's still had over three hundred orphans, many German, although increasingly during the twentieth century the makeup of the home came to reflect the ethnic poor population of Philadelphia. Their care was excellent, given the circumstances of the day.

As of today, St. Vincent's still seeks to continue its mission of helping needy children in Philadelphia. Its record of over 150 years of service to children can be matched by only a few institutions. One can still see the home, reconstructed in its original form after being destroyed by fire in 1980, from the on ramp at the Princeton Avenue entrance going north on I-95. This structure was one of the most impressive sights in Northeast Philadelphia in the 1860s and remains something special to see today.

NORTHEAST SCIENTIST FRANK SHUMAN DISCOVERS SOLAR ENERGY, 1862–1918

One of the most pressing issues in American society today is the energy crisis. Few in the Northeast know that the story of America's fascination with the sun as a power source began at the intersection of Ditman and Disston Streets in Tacony. It was there that Tacony inventor Frank Shuman (1862–1918) developed the first functioning engine driven by the sun.

Frank Shuman was born in Brooklyn, New York, on January 23, 1862, the grandson of a German immigrant. Shuman was bored in the public schools and left elementary school after three years. Always interested in science, Shuman moved to Parkersburg, West Virginia, in 1880 and become a chemist for the dye maker Victor G. Bioede Company. Working at night

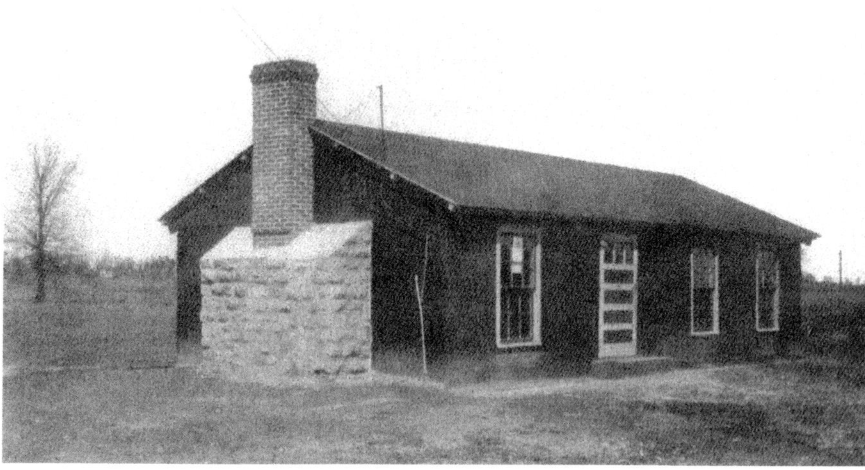

Frank Shuman's laboratory in the open field west of Tacony, where the even side of the 4200 block of Glenside Street is located today. This is where he carried out his experiments with his "Sun Machine." After he died in 1919, his wife gave the cabin to Troop No. 24, the local Boy Scout troop.

on his own, Shuman developed and patented his first invention, a process for making wire glass. When his uncle invited him to Tacony to join the project at Tacony Iron Works to build the statue of William Penn that would be placed on top of city hall, Shuman quickly accepted.

Frank Shuman's wire glass process first gained national notoriety in an issue of *Scientific America* published on November 5, 1892. In the article, Shuman describes the process of melting glass and placing chicken wire in the center of the finished glass plate. Wealthy Philadelphian W.L. Elkins Jr. became interested in the project and financed the American Wire Glass Manufacturing Company in Tacony. For the glass wire invention, Shuman received the prestigious John Scott Medal from the Franklin Institute in Philadelphia. Wire glass was an immediate success, and the invention made Shuman a wealthy man. With this wealth he built an inventors' compound on the city block bordered by Marsden, Longshore, Ditman and Disston Streets in Tacony, landscaped with beautiful gardens. On the lot he built a house for his mother, one for his sister, his own mansion and a laboratory in which he could develop his ideas. Shuman was a workaholic, registering over twenty patents over the next twenty-five years.

In 1906, Shuman became interested in developing what he called a "Sun Machine." It was an outgrowth of his work with wire glass, since he would need a lot of mirrored glass to reflect and increase the heat of the sun. He studied the work of the leaders in the field of solar energy: Frenchman

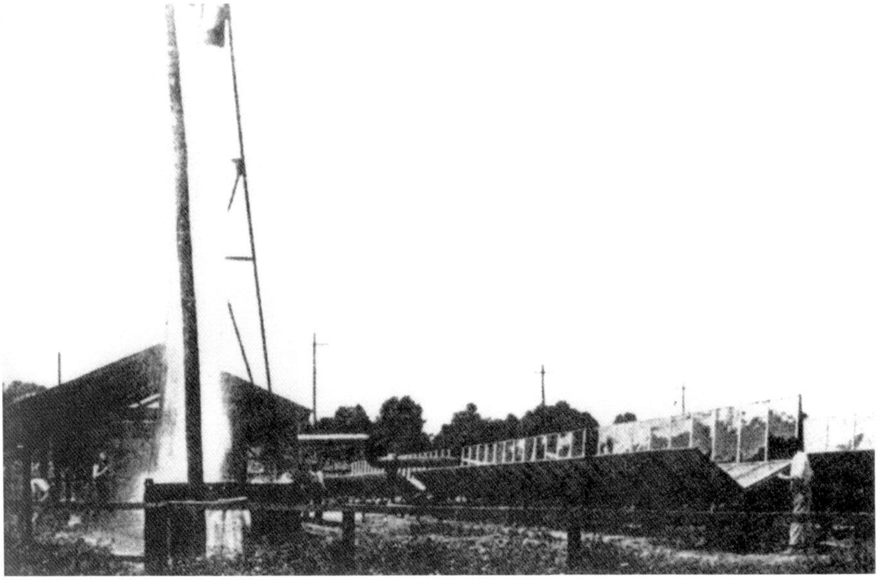

The use of energy produced by the sun first occurred in Tacony in 1912. Shuman's first "Sun Machine" had immovable mirrors that decreased the power of the original machine. The sun reflectors and mirrors provided enough energy to pump the water out of a pipe thirty-three feet high.

Augustin Mouchot and Swede John Ericsson, designer of the Civil War ironclad ship the *Monitor*. But none of their experiments were able to produce enough heat from the sun to run an internal combustion engine. Shuman reached the conclusion that his two predecessors failed because they could not get sufficient steam to run an engine.

Using ether, a liquid with a low boiling point, Shuman set up a series of pipes, mirrors and reflectors so that he could drive a tiny toy steam engine. This, according to Shuman, was America's first successful demonstration of a sun machine. Although his claim was a slight exaggeration, handbills were printed and newspaper advertisements invited anyone interested in seeing the sun drive an engine to come to a demonstration at 4200 Disston Street in Tacony between noon and 3:00 p.m. for the three weeks after August 20, 1907. To the delight of Tacony's children, the machine ran on sunny days throughout the summers of 1908 and 1909.

Working in his Tacony home's laboratory and in a cabin built in the open fields west of Tacony, Shuman made two basic changes to his solar energy machine to try to increase the heat from the sun. First, he increased the number of mirrors to concentrate the sun's rays on a series of long black pipes. By increasing the heat through adjusting the mirrors to always face the sun, Shuman was now able to use water to create steam. Second, since most steam engines were then driven by high-pressure steam, Shuman developed a special low-pressure engine for use with the sun.

From 1809 to 1910, those visiting Shuman's laboratories behind his home witnessed the development of his solar energy engine. Throughout the room were model steam engines, each constructed by Shuman and each model more efficient than the preceding one. Through experimentation he finally found a way to make the emission and exhaust valves on his engine work four times faster than normal. He built a cabin laboratory in the open fields west of the town where he built his first "Sun Machine" model. By 1910, Shuman had developed a workable low-cost, low-pressure steam turbine capable of driving a water pump that could pump three thousand gallons of water per minute and raise it thirty-three feet.

Shuman patented the entire system as a "solar engine designed to convert the sun's heat into energy." Lord Horatio Herbert Kitchener, British war hero of Khartoum and now England's consul-general of Egypt, heard of the new device and knew that it would be ideal for irrigating the Nile Valley and making it an agricultural area. Shuman went to Egypt in 1912 and supervised construction of a successful full scale sun energy plant in Meadi, near Cairo. *Scientific America* lauded Shuman's Egyptian solar plant as "thoroughly practical in every way." Inquiries came from the German government for a plant in their African territories. Shuman spoke of his

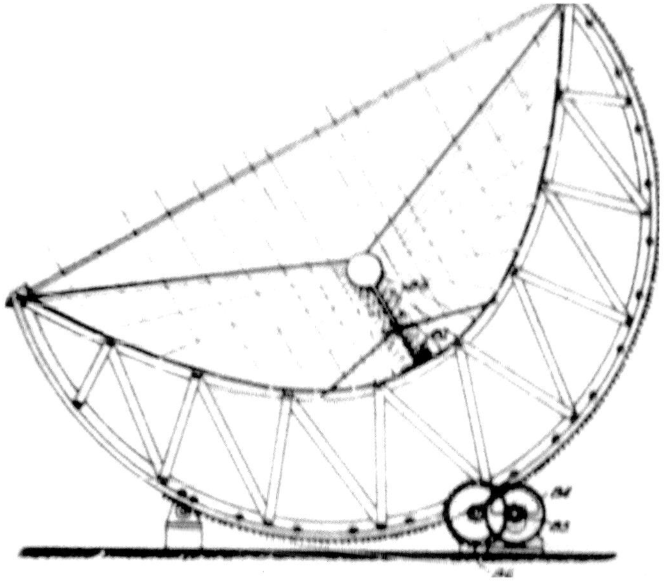

The "Sun Machine" built by Shuman in Egypt contained mirrors and reflectors that were built on frames that could be adjusted to always face the sun. This is Shuman's drawing, which shows how he wanted his frames produced.

invention before the German Reichstag and was presented with a contract for 200,000 deutschmarks for a solar plant in southwest Africa. For these accomplishments Shuman was granted an honorary master of science degree from Cornell University, a degree he refused to accept since he took pride in never being granted a degree by any school.

Unfortunately for Shuman, and the world, the outbreak of World War I in 1914 ended his dream. The European engineers running the Meadi plant left Africa to join the army or do war-related work in their respective homelands, and Shuman went back to the United States. He brought with him the film of the working model of the Meadi sun power plant. Local residents of Northeast Philadelphia were treated to the film of the Meadi operation at the Liberty Movie House on Longshore Street. Mrs. Margaret Dorsey Fairly, a neighbor of Shuman's, remembered with pride the viewing of the Egyptian sun machine at the Liberty Movie House. The movie house was full, and Shuman stayed to answer questions from the audience. It was the talk of Tacony for the next month.

Solar energy development was completely halted by the war. All attention was directed toward the development of the internal combustion gasoline engine for use in cars and airplanes. Cheap oil and the convenience of these engines put solar energy on the back burner.

Shuman's most noteworthy invention that affected today's world occurred in 1916. As part of the American "safety first" movement of 1915, he invented what was then called "Super-Glass." The new glass was made up of two pieces of polished plate glass between which was placed celluloid. The glass and celluloid were welded together under high temperature and tremendous pressure to form a solid glass. Today this invention is still used in trains and cars and is known as safety glass. His untimely death in 1918 came when he was interested in pursuing new work in solar energy, a field that had few supporters.

Frank Shuman was a visionary. He predicted television before radio came on the market. He believed that rockets would one day go to the moon and envisioned the atom as a source of energy. He foresaw a time when fossil fuels would become scarce and solar energy would become one of the world's hopes for sustainable energy. "One thing I feel sure of," he wrote in 1914, "and that is that the human race must finally utilize direct sun or revert to barbarism when oil becomes extinct." Despite Shuman's prediction, cheap oil and the convenience of the internal combustion engine delayed solar energy experiments for almost half a century.

Part III

Mayfair

Boulevard Pools

Between 1929 and the 1960s, the Boulevard Pools were some of the main attractions in Northeast Philadelphia. The Boulevard Pools were begun with the idea of producing entertainment on a "grand scale" in the Northeast. Everything would be bigger and better, with entertainment that would rival anything found elsewhere. It all began in 1926, when famed pool architect William F.B. Koelte began planning a pool for the Northeast. While it would be located in Mayfair, the pool's target clientele would be from the more populated neighborhoods to the south. The two men most responsible for arranging the financing were C. John Birkmann, president of Holmesburg National Bank, and William T. Knauer, special deputy attorney general for the Commonwealth of Pennsylvania. They enlisted the support of a number of factory owners (with businesses small to medium in size) in Kensington and Frankford who were willing to invest in the pool, since having such an attraction nearby would help make their neighborhoods more livable in the summer months. The Boulevard Recreation Company, as the new company was named, raised the necessary funds without much support from the Northeast communities above Frankford. At the time, Roosevelt Boulevard was mostly open lands from Oxford Circle to Pennypack Circle, with few cross streets. For the people of Frankford and Kensington, the pool was in a very convenient location, just a short, pleasant drive up the boulevard. To show how little Koelte knew about the Northeast, he announced that his new pool would open in Tacony at Tyson Street and Roosevelt Boulevard Those familiar with the neighborhood knew that the area was not Tacony.

The Boulevard Pools prepared to open May 30, 1928, with great ceremony. Plans for the opening demonstrated how interested the investors were in attracting Kensington and Frankford residents to the pools. A parade was formed in Womrath Park at Frankford and Kensington Avenues in Frankford, made up mostly of delegates from Kensington and Frankford community and civic groups. A band and bugle contest opened the parade, with Tacony's Oxley Post American Legion Band and Boy Scout Troop 140 Band winning prizes. The parade grew in numbers as it went up Frankford Avenue to Oxford Avenue, west to the boulevard and then to Tyson Street. By the time it reached the pools, the crowd was estimated at four thousand strong.

At the corner of Tyson Street and the boulevard, the marchers were overwhelmed by the sight of a lighthouse, the two acres of pools and by the size of the main building. Erected at a cost of over half a million dollars, the pool was one of the largest and most complete swimming facilities in America. It was composed of four separate compartments that furnished water at varying depths. The diving pool had a ten-foot springboard and a low springboard with a pool depth of ten feet. The main building contained locker rooms for six thousand people, a sixty- by one-hundred-foot ball room on the second floor, a restaurant and restrooms. The entire property covered seven acres, with grandstands surrounding the pools that

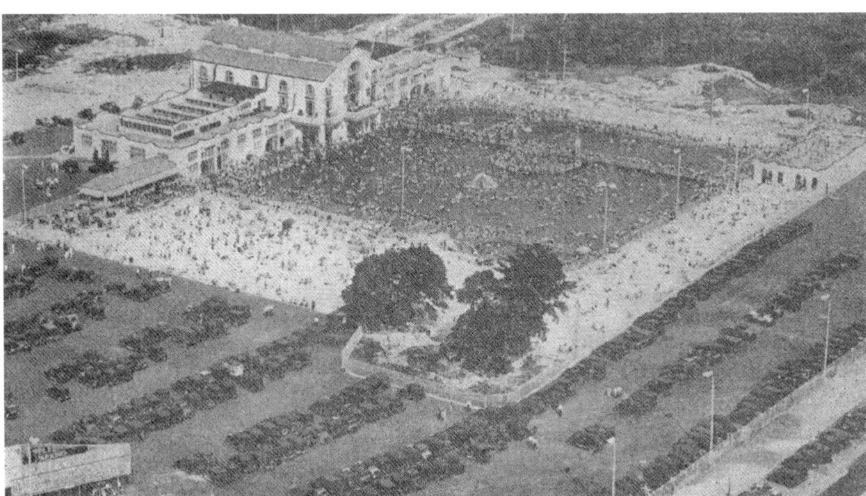

A picture of the Boulevard Pools taken from the Tyson Street and Roosevelt Boulevard corner in 1930. Notice the lighthouse on the corner, the crowds in the pools and the number of cars. The sand around the pool was later removed because it clogged the filtration system.

seated three thousand people for watching water shows, races and thrill-seeking entertainment. Tons of sand were placed around the pool, along with trees and lunch tables, creating what newspapers of the day called "the Northeast's Seashore."

The opening in the 1930s attracted more than 50,000 people to the Boulevard Pools. That Sunday, a crowd of 7,500—avoiding the hot streets of Kensington and Frankford—went to the Boulevard Pools at a cost of twenty-five cents per adult and ten cents per child. Reporters interviewing patrons found people coming from as far away as Norristown, Lancaster, Trenton and even Washington. The entertainment on that weekend consisted of the spectacular diving show of lifeguard Robert Rodgers and the clever water antics of lifeguard clowns Nolan Downing and Jimmy Greaby. The investors were pleased with the success of the pool and their investment.

The staff at the pools consisted of Albert Hoxie, musical director of the Dance Hall; six locker room supervisors; and ten lifeguards (who were all male), paid twenty-five dollars a week for their fourteen weeks of service. The lifeguards could get an extra ten dollars by participating in the aquatic shows. The captain of the lifeguards was Big George Gemas, who was hired to enforce the rules of the pool. To be in charge of a pool in those days meant that you had to enforce the rules without calling for outside help. Not only did Big George swim, but he was also a professional boxer. Everyone knew his reputation as a fighter. In 1930, he knocked out Larry Doyle, a former National Amateur Heavyweight Champion, in his sixteenth consecutive victory.

Much of the success of the pools would be changed by an incident that occurred on August 30, 1930. The season was drawing to a close and attendance was down, so the investors hatched a scheme to increase business. They rented an alligator and advertised a special show, exclaiming, "Come See Our Life Guards Wrestle an Alligator at Boulevard Pools on August 30, 1930."

On that day some 1,500 spectators filled the stands to see the event. Robert Rogers, who lived at 3419 Friendship Street in Mayfair and was the lifeguard diver who often volunteered to be in the pool's aquatic shows, opted to wrestle the alligator for a weeks' pay of twenty-five dollars. The alligator was to have its mouth tied closed with a rope, and Robert was to pick him out of two feet of water and throw him on his back during the fifteen-minute exhibition—no easy task with a ten foot alligator that weighed 150 pounds. Rogers was in the pool ready to begin when he reached for the alligator's head, but as he pulled back, the rope around its mouth came loose. The alligator, realizing he was free, opened his mouth, exposing his razor-sharp

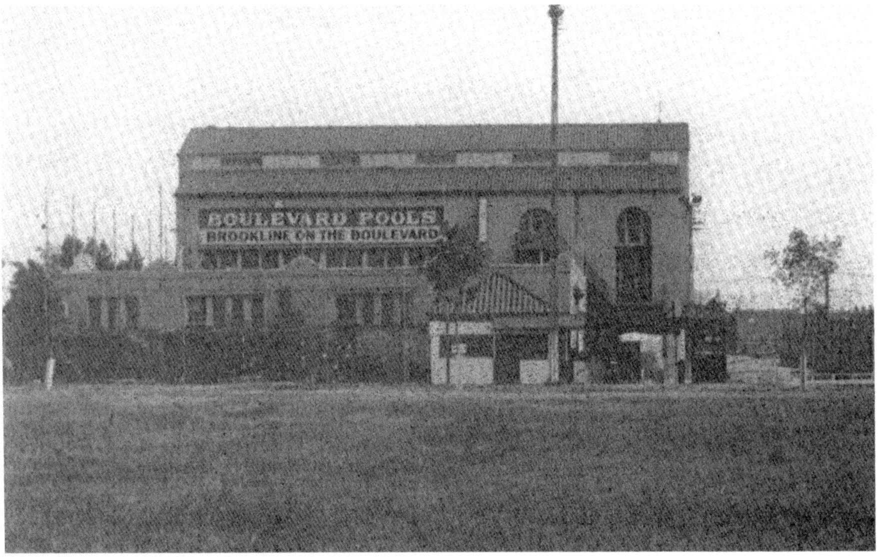

The Roosevelt Pools, taken from Roosevelt Boulevard in 1950.

teeth and went after Robert, who was bitten on his hand as he hollered for help. His brother, nineteen-year-old George Rogers, hearing his brother call for help, jumped into the pool and began pulling the alligator away from him. In the struggle the alligator bit into George's left hand and arm, causing great bleeding. The crowd was in shock, screaming in horror. The alligator was shot as George left the pool holding a towel over his left side. Despite his agony, George grinned at the crowd, then ran to the first-aid stand, where he collapsed. He was carried to a car and taken to Frankford Hospital, where his left hand and arm were amputated inches below the elbow. Four weeks later at a workman's compensation board hearing, George Rogers was awarded $2,792.50 for the loss of his arm, while his brother Robert was paid $211.36 for the injuries he suffered. As was often the case in those days, no legal action was taken against the Boulevard Recreation Corporation, but they were openly criticized by the compensation board.

What had started out as a way to increase attendance and offer more spectacular shows only served to decrease attendance for the remainder of the year. What mother would send her children to a pool that had alligators? Negative rumors spread throughout the community about the type of entertainment at the pool, causing the owners to plan an opening in 1931 with less reliance on entertainment and more emphasis on having the public swim in the pool. The rentals of the dance hall for parties and wedding receptions also became a reliable source of revenue for the owners.

A final rejection of the grand style of entertainment originally envisioned for the pool came with the removal of the sand later in the 1930s. It had become too expensive to continually clean the sand out of the filter pumps. By the 1940s and '50s, the Boulevard Pools had evolved into a "swim club," with members paying yearly or daily fees. The idea of the founders to have "grand scale" entertainment at the pools filled with thrills and danger had died with the alligator.

PREPARING FOR WAR: MAYFAIR IN 1941

The Mayfair community stands in marked contrast to Tacony in its reaction to federal intervention at the start of World War II. Government-funded improvements to the Disston Saw Company were supported enthusiastically by Tacony citizens, while government funding for workers' housing was not embraced by the Mayfair community.

The controversy began in 1940, when government officials realized that if the war came, additional workers would be needed for the factories located along the Delaware River. Disston's new armor plate plant would require an additional one hundred workers. The projected need for Disston's Saw Company and the Frankford Arsenal was eight thousand workers. Workers moving into the area would need affordable housing in Mayfair if the factory jobs were to be filled.

There were laws on the books, used during the Depression, to fund low-cost housing. These laws were amended in October 1940 to include wartime defense workers' housing as well. Lawrence Westbrook, director of the Federal Works Agency's Mutual Ownership Defense Housing Division, used this act to initiate the building of homes for defense workers. One of the sites chosen was Northeast Philadelphia. The specific location was to be on the grounds of the Lower Dublin Poor House in the newly formed community of Mayfair. The government secretly received the go-ahead from the city to use this Fairmount Park land as a building site. However, news leaked out to the public, and community organizations in Mayfair planned a public protest for June 18, 1941.

Much of the talk in the community was about the loss of property values The claim was that the homes for which residents paid over $5,000 (the actual cost was a little over $4,000) would be competing against $3,000 public housing units. Renters would be charged $22 a month, which included taxes and all utilities. This seemed unfair to Mayfair homeowners, who got no such relief. Rumors regarding who was going to live in the homes and what

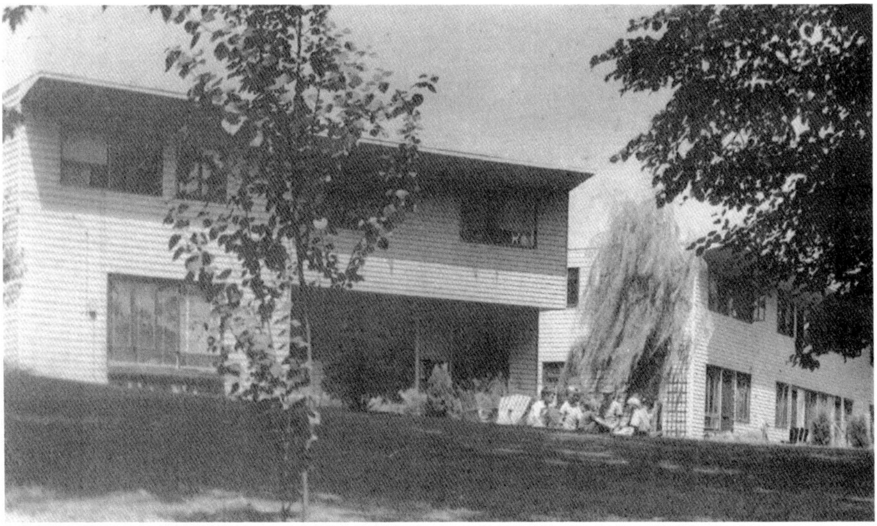

A Pennypack Woods home built in 1941 for civil defense workers. Vinyl siding was added in the 1960s, as shown in this picture.

it would mean to the lifestyle of their community also surfaced. Word of mouth spread these fears throughout the community, guaranteeing a large turnout for "the protest" meeting.

On the morning of June 18, over 1,200 people gathered at the Mayfair Athletic Association baseball field at Ryan and Rowland Avenues. Presiding over the meeting was John T. Ginhart of 3521 Aldine Street, president of the Mayfair Athletic Association. Ginhart thanked the people for their support and then introduced John J. Nesbitt, president of the Mayfair Improvement Association, who professed his dislike of public housing no matter what the reason for its use. City Councilman Clarence Crossan followed with a forceful speech against the project. He pointed out that the "government would pay only the equivalent of 15% of tax paid by Mayfair householders," adding that the government did not need the Mayfair site. Councilman Frank Egan followed, further exciting the crowd. "National Defense housing is needed but doesn't mean that self-respecting communities and self-respecting Americans must pay for projects to support other Americans." Jacob Boonin, chairman of the transportation committee of the Mayfair Improvement Association, outlined the community's objections to the proposal, stating that "thousands of row homes, mostly new, in this section, pay more taxes per square foot than any other section of the city." In an effort to calm the situation, Federal Housing Representative G. Gersham Griggs invited all parties to lunch at the Torresdale Country Club after a tour of Mayfair, which had been scheduled previously.

At the lunch meeting, Councilman Crossan, clutching petitions from the community, told Griggs that he would sponsor a law that prohibited the federal government from using the land at Ryan and Rowland Avenues for housing for defense workers. Two days later, the federal government announced that one thousand homes for defense workers would be built in the sparsely developed area on Frankford Avenue between Holme Avenue and St. Dominic Church. The people of Mayfair were ecstatic. The project was to begin within the week with a completion date set for six months. The people of Mayfair had saved parkland for future use. (The land was used to build Lincoln High School in 1948.)

The building of the government project was yet another issue. WPA labor was used for grading, laying out streets and curbs and all other outside work. No building permits were issued by the city because that process would have slowed the project. This angered Carroll Shelton, president of the Philadelphia Builders Association, who charged that the project of wood frame units was a "firetrap and in violation of municipal codes." Another builder complained that the plumbing used for the project had "a code all its own." None of this mattered after December 7, 1941, when the necessities of war overrode civilian concerns. However, all these issues remained when the property was taken over by the Pennypack Woods Homeowners Association after the war.

Of most interest in this story is that the Mayfair community was not convinced that war with Germany was inevitable. Mayfair opted for a community unchanged by federal projects. To Mayfair residents, open space and protecting the value of their property were more important than national defense efforts by the federal government. They opted to keep what they had rather than prepare for a war that might not happen. Yet, less than a mile southeast of Mayfair lay Tacony, the national "poster community" for all-out war.

THE NAMING OF LINCOLN HIGH SCHOOL, 1949–1950

The current construction of a contemporary Abraham Lincoln High School at Ryan and Rowland Avenues provides us an opportunity to reflect on the construction of the original Lincoln High School in 1949.

With the end of World War II in 1945, the building of air light row homes (a reference to roomier interior layouts) exploded throughout the Mayfair community. They were crowded together on small streets east of Frankford Avenue, selling for less than $9,000. On the west side, the streets remained slightly wider, and the houses sold for $10,000. The last home in an air

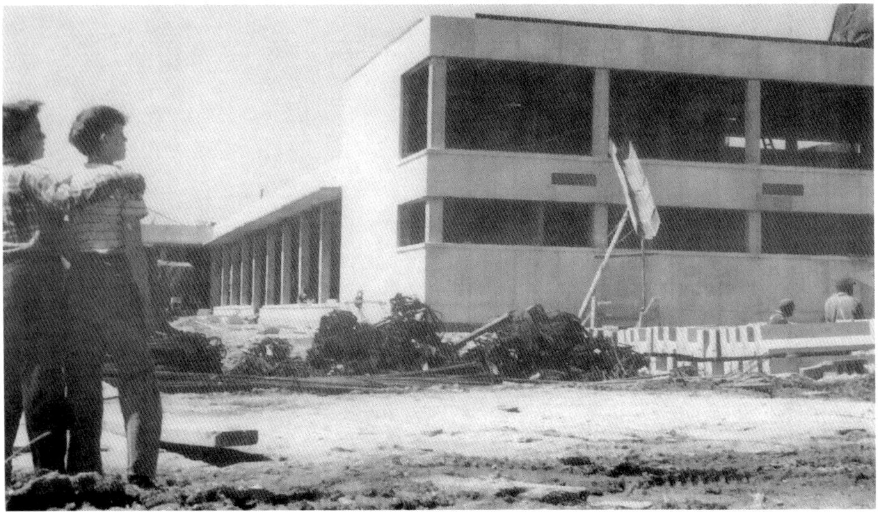

In the spring of 1949, the new school at Ryan and Rowland Avenues was called Mayfair High School. Two neighborhood boys watch the school being built. The school opened in February 1950, only halfway finished.

light row usually featured offices that were occupied by lawyers, doctors and dentists. The area around Frankford and Cottman saw the opening of new appliance stores, large food markets, real estate offices and television repair shops. Everything that was needed was nearby. Realtors advertising homes found that this new neighborhood attracted a higher price than the older homes in Holmesburg and Tacony. It became the practice to advertise homes in the Holmesburg and Tacony communities as being in Mayfair.

The original pressure on the school board to build the school came from the Mayfair Improvement Association. They recommended the Rowland and Ryan Avenues site that was left vacant by a 1941 public housing dispute. The plan and location won approval without much public notice. The decision to build the school exacerbated feelings between the three communities. Holmesburg was by far the oldest community, with many residents having lived there for over sixty years. Tacony, a factory town begun by Henry Disston in 1872, was inhabited mostly by English and Irish steel makers and their families. Mayfair was made up mostly of people who had moved from Kensington, Olney and South Philadelphia. Each of these communities had different ideas of what the new school should be named. The proposed school was originally called "Mayfair High School" by those planning the building, since every recently built high school in Philadelphia had been named after a neighborhood. The assumption by the board was that this policy would continue. Charles H. Williams, principal of Benjamin Franklin High School, was named principal of the new school and given the task of opening it. The process was interrupted when a group of Holmesburg residents concerned over the school's name asked for a hearing with the school board.

At the meeting, it became clear that the three communities closest to the school had different ideas as to what the school should be named. As one Holmesburg resident said, "There is no such community as 'Mayfair,' it is nothing more than a builder's trade name." The Tacony community was less vocal, but let it be known that the Henry Disston family had donated land in 1936 at the current Vogt Playground site for the Jacob Disston High School. The school was not built because of the Depression, and the site was still vacant. Given this gift, the community felt that the new high school should be built in Tacony and named for the founders of the community, the Disston family. Nevertheless, Mayfair residents insisted that the school be named after their community. They may not be a historic community, but they felt that they were the community of the future.

The school board, in private session, sensing the deep split in the communities over the issue, chose a name no patriotic American could find objectionable—Abraham Lincoln High School. Who could find fault in naming a school after one of America's greatest presidents? But Mayfair leader Thomas Donahue did. "We're proud of our community. Why should this school be named for Lincoln or any other man?" Mrs. Adeline Welsh of Mayfair added, "We're proud and disappointed by the switch. We're going to do everything we can to fight it. It's just an example of jealousy on the part of some of the older communities." Mrs. Thomas B. Everest of the Holmesburg Association objected, stating that "everybody had an opportunity to submit a name. Abraham Lincoln's was one of the several submitted by Holmesburg. Why all the fuss? The main thing is that the whole section will have a high school."

Unable to change the school board's position on the name Abraham Lincoln High School, Donahue and the Mayfair Association took the case to court on September 19, 1949. In one of the rare lawsuits ever filed over the naming of a school, Judges George Gowen Parry and Joseph L. Kin ruled in favor of the school board, criticizing the motives of those in Mayfair who objected to the name Abraham Lincoln. The citation from the ruling was as follows:

> *As much as the plaintiffs and many other residents of the Mayfair section are to be admired for the strong sense of local pride, they show an utterly untenable conviction of the purpose of a public educational system. Such a system is not intended to promote the business or economic interest in any locality.*

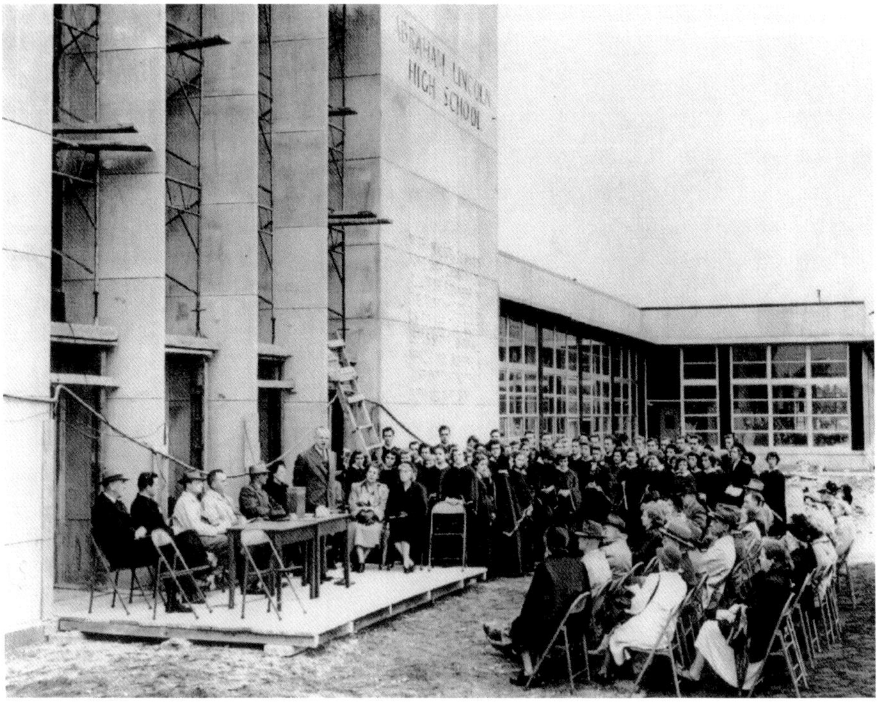

Ceremonies at the official opening of Lincoln High School in January 1950. By this time, the legal bickering between communities had ended. The school was officially named Abraham Lincoln High School.

After the decision, Donahue and his followers were informed in private session by the school board that the planned elementary school to be built at St. Vincent and Hawthorn Streets would be called Mayfair Elementary School. The dispute was settled, but the issue raised by these Northeast Philadelphia communities did change school policy. In the past, the names of high schools had reflected the community in which they were built. Schools such as Frankford High, Overbrook High, West Philadelphia High, Kensington High, Olney High and Roxbourgh High were named after their local communities. From now on, high schools would be named not for neighborhoods but after famous Americans like George Washington and Thomas Edison.

The feud over Lincoln High reflects historic developments in each of the three neighborhoods. The proud people of Holmesburg simply did not like the idea of a new community, carved out of their boundaries, lending its name to the new high school in their original territory. Taconyites felt just as strongly about the use of the name "Mayfair," especially since the city had taken ground from the Disston family years before and never fulfilled its commitment to build the Jacob Disston High School. Ultimately, the real estate industry had the final say. Mayfair had newer homes, with parking spaces for cars in the rear. Everyone was buying cars in the postwar period, unlike the war years when they were not produced in quantities. This was a very attractive perk to home buyers after the war. Tacony became "Lower Mayfair," and homes in Holmesburg were advertised as being in Mayfair, blotting out the uniqueness of each of these early communities. Today, the name Mayfair has largely triumphed, encompassing much of the areas formerly called Holmesburg and Tacony.

As one looks back at the dispute over the proposed name—Mayfair High School—for the new school at Ryan and Rowland Avenues, it is not difficult to imagine a future that included Burholme High School (Northeast High School) and Somerton High School (Washington High School). The name Lincoln High School was a clear victory by the school district over local control and input by local communities, a trend which continues to define school issues today.

THE "OLD" LINCOLN HIGH SCHOOL, 1950–2009

The new high school to be built in Northeast Philadelphia in 1949 was projected to be the jewel of the Philadelphia school system. As the first school built in Philadelphia after World War II, it was designed and constructed to be what reformers described as a community school. All previous high schools, with the exception of Central High School and Girls High School, catered to specific communities of Frankford, Overbrook, Germantown, South Philadelphia, West Philadelphia and Roxborough. Because the Northeast was projected to be a high-population area, the new school would require space to hold large numbers of students, including classrooms, community rooms and gymnasiums that required many entrances and bathrooms for thousands of students.

It was also to be the first community school built to meet emergencies during the Cold War. Included in the plans was a design that allowed the school to become a community hospital in case of a nuclear attack. Ramps, not steps, were built to get from one floor to the next. Large hallways with many entrances were designed to be able to transport the injured to makeshift hospital rooms. An extra-large number of restrooms were included in the plans. The basement of the school was filled with canned goods and medical supplies, including drugs, for use in civil defense emergencies. The gym had stands for 4,000 and the auditorium for 1,500. The community room could

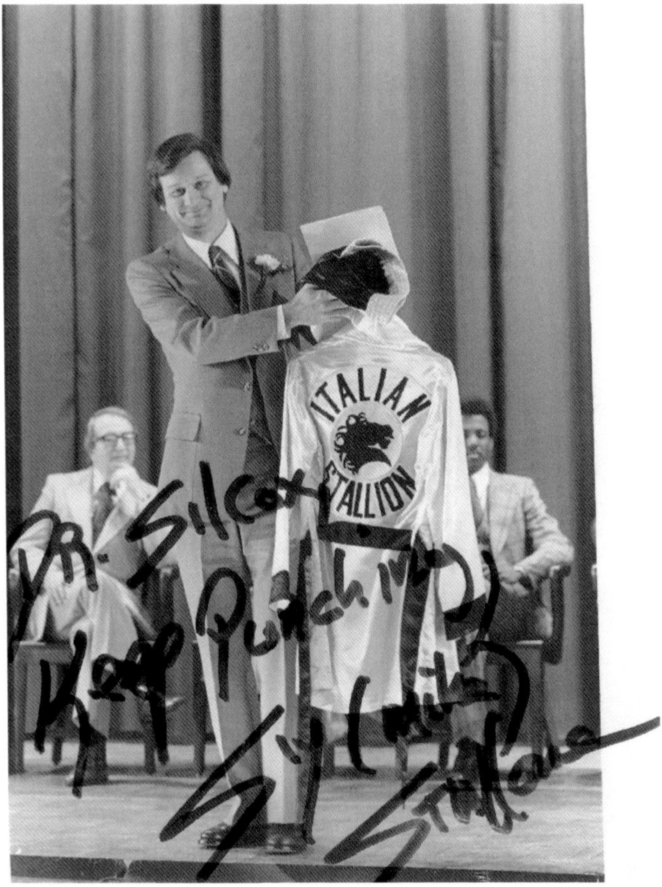

The principal accepts the boxer trunks and robe used in the movie *Rocky II* and a check for $10,000 given by Sylvester Stallone for the school's student activity fund. Notice that the picture contains a message for the principal.

hold 1,000 people for luncheons. Handball courts and a sixty-four-acre field provided for sports activity. The fields were to be made available to the community without cost.

In 1949, Charles H. Williams was named the school's principal. Williams was an academic scholar and English major who had been the principal of Benjamin Franklin High School. He had gained a reputation as a strong and fair leader for his untiring work at Franklin. He was able to put together the best department heads and teachers for the faculty of the new school. Unfortunately, because of overcrowding—at Frankford High at Oxford and Wakeling; Northeast High School for Boys at Eighth and Lehigh; and the few available elementary schools in the area—space had to be found for children of the new homeowners in the Northeast as soon as possible. Williams was pressured by the school administration to open the school before it was completed.

So it was that in February 1950, the first students entered the new high school. Lincoln was designated a junior-senior high school, grades seven through twelve. The gym, auditorium and a number of classrooms had not been completed. Large canvas sheets were placed at the ends of most hallways. The rooms that were completed were warm, but on cold, windy March days students moved quickly through the chilly hallways to get to their next class. Workmen were on the school grounds, and the sounds of construction reverberated throughout the building. The school was finished by September 1950, and the first class of seventy-two students graduated in June 1951. Lincoln entered the Public League that first year and initiated an era of outstanding sports teams.

By 1957, the school contained a student body of seventh- to twelfth-grade students that numbered 5,500. It was at the time the largest high school in Pennsylvania. In its early years, Lincoln High provided the community with many school events, and local residents turned out in large numbers to support the school. The great basketball team of 1952–53 sold out University of Pennsylvania's home court, Palestra, during its loss to Wilt Chamberlain's Overbrook team. The "City Champion" 1958 Lincoln football team drew a crowd of 45,000 to the championship game against LaSalle High School at Frankllin Field. In 1965, the Public League Championship basketball team led by Larry Cannon drew crowds of 3,000 to the gym for its games and 7,000 to the Palestra for the City Championship game. Yearly jamborees consisting of gymnastics and large rhythmic groups drew sold-out crowds of 4,000 to the school, and school shows were attended by 1,500 people per night. Everything about the school was big.

The population in Northeast Philadelphia continued to grow in the post–World War II years. The solution was to build more schools. A new Northeast high school was built at Cottman and Algon Streets in 1958. This relieved Lincoln of all students west of Roosevelt Boulevard. Lincoln's population declined to 4,400 students. The opening of Washington High School in the Far Northeast in 1963 served the growing population in that area and allowed Lincoln's population to remain at 4,400. The school functioned without incident in this period and featured many high-caliber educational programs. It was selected by the University of Pittsburgh to house a multimillion-dollar computer system, the first in Pennsylvania. The school also offered accelerated college programs in every academic field.

All of this was done under the leadership of Charles H. Williams. His retirement in 1970 represented the end of an era. His successor was Dr. Bernard Rafferty, then principal at Harding Jr. High School. In 1971, the school was hit with a drug scandal caused by the very drugs left in the basement for the community when the school was built. Somehow students had gotten a set of keys to the basement. In their explorations, they found the morphine pills left in 1950 for civil defense purposes. They began selling them throughout the school. Albert Buck, lead nonteaching assistant at the time, uncovered the scheme. Police were summoned and the drugs removed. The story became a headline in all Philadelphia newspapers for weeks, however. It also ushered in a new issue for all schools—a drug culture involving young people. Managing large schools became a challenge. Suddenly, small seemed better.

Dr. Harry C. Silcox became principal in 1976 and served until 1992. Silcox was a member of the first graduating class in 1951, basketball star at Temple (1951–55), basketball coach at Lincoln (1957–67) and vice-principal (1967–76). He lived in the neighborhood, understanding the school and the community. In one of the most exciting days in the school's history, he welcomed back former student Sylvester Stallone, who produced a scene in the school auditorium for *Rocky II*. Before 1,700 enthusiastic students, Stallone presented the school with the black and gold robe and boxing trunks worn in *Rocky II* and a check for $10,000 for the student activity fund.

In 1978, a swimming pool was added next to the Ryan Avenue parking lot for community use. A year later, an asbestos crisis hit the school, since it had been built with plaster mixed with asbestos as an acoustical sound barrier. The school was closed for three months in the 1980s for repair. All of the asbestos-covered walls were carpeted to seal them, while the ceilings were left uncovered but had to be checked daily for roof leaks. Asbestos still remains an issue for the soon-to-be-dismantled school.

Court-ordered desegregation was enacted in 1979. The ruling eliminated the old boundary rule that required students to live in the school's immediate area. The community school was now a citywide school. New specialized programs were introduced, and the school became a center for the hearing-impaired, horticultural programs, environmental programs and Air Force ROTC. Under the leadership of David Kipphut, these programs became nationally recognized, and the environmental students were invited to the first People to People Environmental Conference in Moscow in 1988.

Despite all of these efforts to improve the school, the open boundary policy led to fewer and fewer neighborhood students in the school population. The school was too spread out, too large and too unmanageable for the world of the twenty-first century. At a community meeting in 2004, it was decided to tear down the old school and build a new, smaller and more compact school. This new school is being built at the time of this writing. We can only hope that it is constructed for a smaller student body and designed to function as a good neighbor for the community.

Part IV

Bustleton/Somerton/Byberry

Bustleton: Part of the First Air Mail Service Route in the United States

As airplane flights began to become common in the United States in the early years of the twentieth century, landing fields in Philadelphia were frequently discussed. Very little was done about it until 1918. On February 12 of that year, an announcement was made that an air mail service route was about to be established between Washington and New York, with a station in Philadelphia to be used for refueling and a mail stop. Postal officials and officers from the U.S. Aviation Service, together with a Philadelphia delegation, toured the city on February 21, 1918, looking for a landing site. On February 26, the group announced that League Island Park in South Philadelphia had been selected for the landing field. A week later the city turned down the site because it needed the site to dump coal ashes then being discarded by Philadelphia residents, most of whom had coal-fired furnaces. Finally, a 137-acre site near Byberry, Red Lion Roads and Bensalem Pike (Roosevelt Boulevard) in Bustleton was chosen for the landing field.

While much was happening in Washington, the people of Bustleton noticed little difference in their long established farming community. Not much was needed to prepare the landing field, except to roll the field to keep it flat, keep the grass cut short and build a small wooden building that would became the U.S. Mail Station. Meanwhile, in Washington, Congress appropriated $100,000 on March 1, 1918, to start the United States Air Mail service route between New York, Philadelphia and Washington. Pressure from the banking industry pushed Congress into faster action. Banks wanted

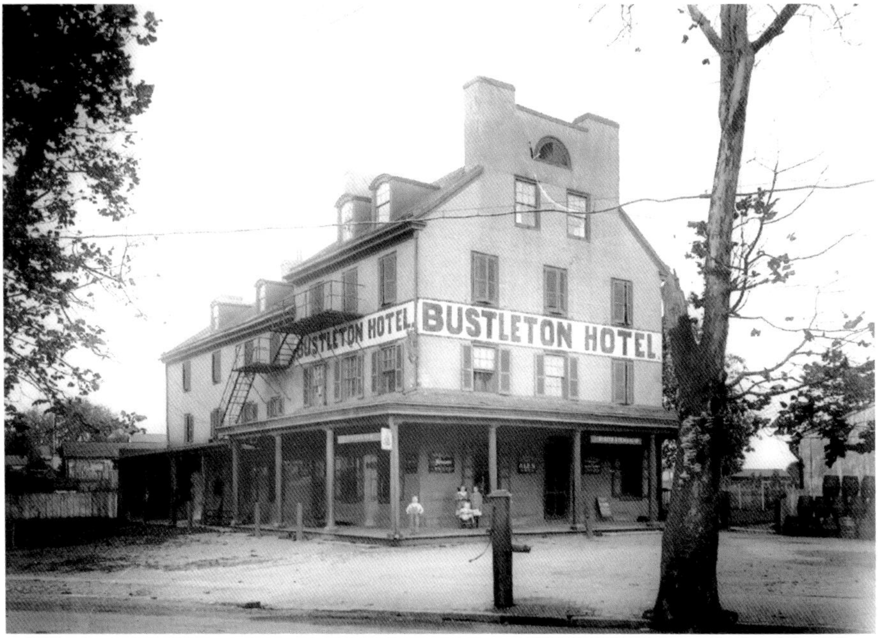

The Bustleton Hotel was filled with flyers, including Colonel Flint, on May 14, 1918, the night prior to the first air mail deliveries in the United States. The building was taken down in 1931.

to cut the "float" time it took to get checks sent between cities, for the faster the checks moved the more money they made. To speed up getting the service into operation, U.S. Army colonel E.A. Deeds decided that army pilots should be ordered to fly the mail because it would be "good training for them."

The three landing fields selected were Belmont Park in New York, the polo field in Potomac Park, Washington, D.C., and Bustleton Field in Philadelphia—all to be used for refueling and the transfer of mailbags. U.S. Army major Reuben H. Fleet was placed in charge of the project at the end of April 1918, but to his surprise he was ordered on May 1 to implement the service on May 15, 1918. That gave him two weeks to select pilots and identify planes capable of flying from Philadelphia to New York or Washington. Fleet asked for a postponement since he estimated that the task of getting all pieces of the operation together would take months. Postmaster General Albert S. Burleson would not consider Fleet's request, stating that the date had been announced to the press and that "even if the war effort had to suffer" the air mail service would begin May 15, 1918. That ended all discussion about a postponement.

Fleet ordered six new Curtiss "Jenny" biplanes without front seats or front controls but with a hopper arrangement in their place for mailbags. The planes were delivered on May 13 to Belmont Park still in their crates, and Fleet and the pilots worked the next seventy-two hours straight to assemble, service, warm up and flight check the aircrafts. On May 14, three planes left Belmont for Bustleton to prepare for the opening of the air mail service. Fleet's plane ran out of gas and landed in the open fields of Northeast Philadelphia, two miles from the Bustleton field. He got a ride to the airfield from a farmer and had another pilot return with gas to fly the plane to the field.

The sleepy town of Bustleton awoke to a beehive of activity on May 14, 1918. Although local residents knew little of the events in Washington, their small dirt roads were filled with gasoline trucks, army personnel in a mail truck and three newly arrived Curtiss "Jenny" biplanes with fresh U.S. Mail signs painted on their sides. People began to gather from near and far to see what was happening. They were surprised to see Major Fleet himself, the man in charge of the operation, at their small airfield. He rented a room at the Bustleton Hotel and spent the night. The thought that Bustleton must be on the verge of something important for the nation filled the conversation in the hotel.

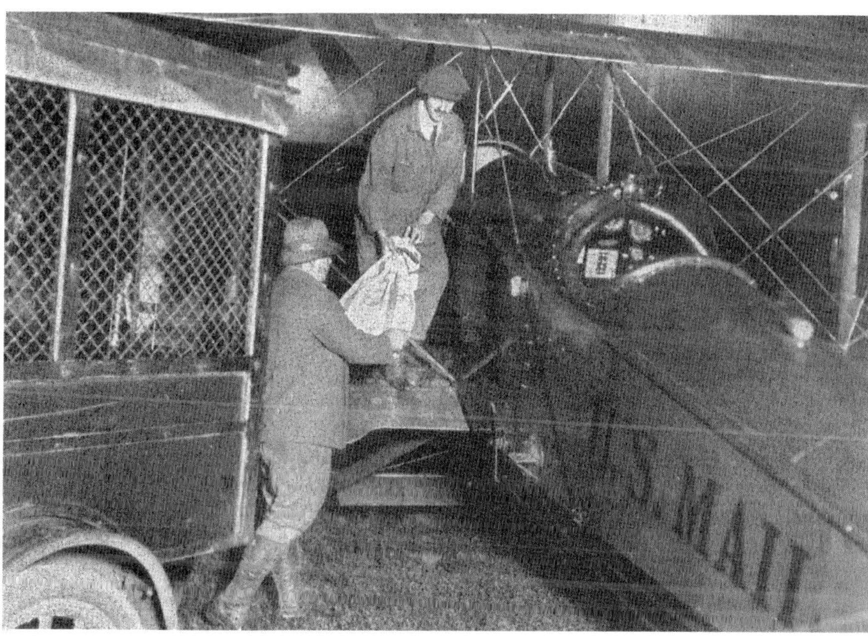

Bustleton on May 15, 1918. Lieutenant Torrey Webb unloads mail for Philadelphia from New York into a truck that will take it to Philadelphia's center city post office. It is the first U.S. Air Mail service delivered in the United States.

May 15, 1918, began in Bustleton with a roar from the engines of a "Jenny" taking off at 8:40 a.m. for Washington, D.C., with Major Fleet at the controls. He was scheduled to be in Washington with President and Mrs. Woodrow Wilson, Assistant Secretary of the Navy (and future president) Franklin D. Roosevelt and other dignitaries to initiate the first air mail flight service in the United States. Fleet could relax now that everything was set. One plane was in Washington ready to go to Philadelphia, one in New York ready to go to Philadelphia and two in Bustleton ready for the return flights to New York and Washington.

In Bustleton, a large crowd had gathered to await Lieutenant Torrey Webb, who was bringing to Philadelphia from New York its first ever mail delivery by airplane. Carrying 149 letters from New York weighing seventy pounds, he left Belmont Park at 11:15 a.m. and arrived at Bustleton's air mail station at 1:00 p.m. Six minutes later, Lieutenant James C. Edgerton took off with letters destined for Washington, while a mail truck laden with the Philadelphia mail was on its way to North Philadelphia Station, where the letters were to be relayed to the center city post office. The northbound air service out of Washington experienced difficulty when the plane got lost and landed twenty-five miles south of that city. Lieutenant Howard P. Calver was waiting at Bustleton to receive the Washington mail, but upon hearing of the mishap he left for New York with only Philadelphia's mail. He arrived in New York at 4:30 p.m. A later review of the first day of mail service revealed the Bustleton airfield service to be the most efficient. The arrival and departure of mail service twice a day became something the community could tell time by. This daily routine became a part of life in Bustleton for the next three years. After its startup, this air mail service to Bustleton appears to have continued daily until 1922, when it was moved to a newly opened airport on Island Road near Tinicum Avenue. The Bustleton field would not be used again until the William Penn Airport opened on that site in 1928.

To coincide with the opening of its air mail service, the postal service began selling air mail stamps the day the service was inaugurated. It cost twenty-four cents for a stamp to cover the expense of the Washington–New York air route, while the cost of regular mail was two cents. It was reported on that day that Philadelphia's main post office sold more than ten thousand of these air mail stamps. Pressed to get the stamps out, one sheet of one hundred air mail stamps with the image of the Curtiss "Jenny" flying upside down got past inspectors.

An alert stamp collector who recognized the misprint bought the entire sheet for twenty-four dollars at the local post office. In the years that followed, the sheet was sold at least twice at handsome profits, then was divided by the buyer into blocks of stamps as well as singles.

Today, if you find an old family letter with an inverted "Jenny" stamp, it is worth more than $250,000, though a recent auction of a pristine stamp brought nearly $1 million for the coveted "Jenny."

In addition to these prized stamps, a second unexpected outcome of the air mail flights brought German immigrant Ernest Buehl to Bustleton. The postal service, eager to improve safety, purchased fifteen Junker planes from Germany in 1920. To service the planes, it hired Buehl, who was then chief engineer in charge of building airplane engines at the BMW Company in Germany. Serving as the chief engineer of the U.S. Postal Service, Buehl visited Bustleton for the first time in 1921. After an adventurous career—he was to become one of America's most notable flyers, adventurers and characters in aviation in the 1920s—he chose to settle down in Bustleton in 1929. He then became a prominent local figure who influenced aviation in Northeast Philadelphia for decades.

AVIATION ENTHUSIAST ERNEST BUEHL AND THE FLYING DUTCHMAN AIRPORT

Little remembered in the history of Northeast Philadelphia is Ernest Buehl. Yet in his time he was considered by those who lived in Bustleton as a charismatic, Damon Runyon–type figure who greatly influenced local citizens into supporting and accepting aviation as the wave of the future. Buehl was normally quiet and respectful, but his German accent became more pronounced and his voice louder as he got into one of his famous stories about his experiences in aviation. In any discussion, it was not long before he took out his flying license No. 824, signed by Orville Wright, and asked his inquisitor, "And who taught you to fly?"

Ernest Buehl came to America in 1920 after serving in the German air force in World War I. He was a mechanic hired by BMW after the war to supervise the production of aircraft engines. Economic times were hard in Germany, so when he was asked to take a similar job for the U.S. Aviation Service, he accepted and moved to America. His work with the air mail service planes brought him to Bustleton in 1920. He met a girl there who he would later marry. But settling down at that time was not for him. His adventurous nature prompted him to accept an offer from the air mail service to be part of the team attempting to establish the first air mail service route from New York to San Francisco in 1921. The pilot and leader of the team was Bert Acosta, assisted by young Eddie Rickenbacker, who volunteered to be the copilot. The head mechanic of the team was Buehl, who was responsible for adding extra

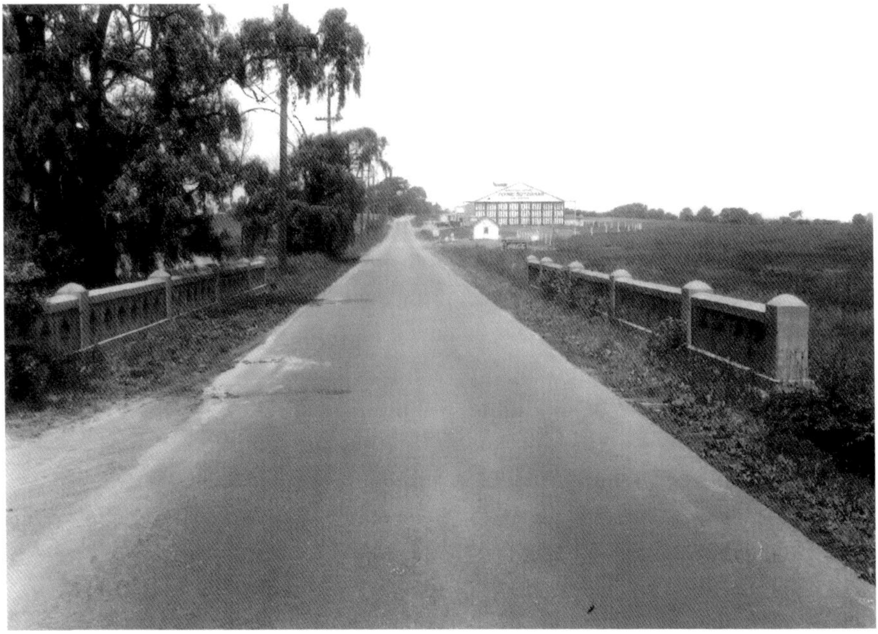

A rare picture of the Flying Dutchman Airfield in Bustleton in 1935. The field was owned by Ernest Buehl and identified his German background. The photo was taken on Comly Road, looking south on Bustleton Avenue.

fuel tanks to the plane for the long trip. Decades later, as Rickenbacker's fame grew, Buehl always found a story to tell about his friend.

At the time, air mail service was the most dangerous work possible. Out of the first forty pilots hired, twenty died in air crashes. For this reason, Buehl left the air service to fly for explorer Roald Amundsen on one of his trips to the North Pole. He was then hired to provide supplies for the expedition then camped at Fort Norman near the North Pole. The flight from Edmonton to Fort Normal was extremely dangerous and quite uncomfortable. His engine was water cooled and needed to run so as not to freeze, and the plane's open cabin structure gave him no warmth except for the heavy fur-lined clothes he wore. After a couple of years in the air postal service and hearing of the deaths of 50 percent of the air mail pilots, Buehl quit. In 1927, his wealth consisting of just one plane, he returned to Bustleton and married his sweetheart.

He flew out of the old mail field at Boulevard airfield for a couple of years to earn additional money. By 1929, Buehl had two planes and enough wealth to purchase two hundred acres of flat, open land at Bustleton and Tomlinson Roads. The drainage of the ground was checked, the fields dragged and rolled and the airfield was put into use. On November 4, 1929, Buehl built a hangar for eight planes, renting space for three planes to three of his former flying students. The "Flying Dutchman Air Service" thus began three decades of air service in Bustleton. Offering aerial photography, topography, advertising, student flight instruction, cross-country and passenger flights, the service never lacked for business. He became the prototype of the many American private pilots who conducted flying schools in the 1930s. The Flying Dutchman, as the airfield came to be called, first appeared in the Philadelphia Chamber of Commerce Aviation Map of 1930, where it was shown as a 115-acre irregular field of sod with a circular airport symbol in the center. The buildings on the airfield were modest—one metal and one wooden hangar used for storage or engine repair for those garaging their planes. There were no towers to oversee landings and takeoffs, and only a wind flag to help pilots with wind directions.

By 1932, Buehl had moved his home to Willow Grove and was known to all in the Northeast as the Flying Dutchman. He then applied for and received a certificate of public conveyance to fly out of Bustleton as a common carrier between Philadelphia and towns in Pennsylvania. During the 1930s, Buehl taught over three thousand Northeast Philadelphians to fly and traveled thousands of miles transporting people from Northeast Philadelphia. His last flight was in 1986, when he was in his eighties. Anyone who ever took a flying lesson with him never forgot the experience. He had a story for every occasion. George Brown recounted his first flight lesson from Buehl: "When you did something he thought was bad he would fly you over a cemetery and point towards the ground. He'd say, see if you don't do what I tell you, that's where you'll end up."

In May 1941 Buehl was made to share his field space with the "Brewster Flying Club." Organized by the workers the Brewster Aircraft Plant in nearby Johnsville, Pennsylvania, they operated out of Flying Dutchman Air Field with special permission from the U.S. government. When the war ended, a great housing boom encompassed the Northeast. Buehl realized that he could not keep the field any longer. The Flying Dutchman Air Field land was sold to builders in 1953 for a large housing development. By 1955, the airport had disappeared from the map of the area, with houses filling the space formerly occupied by the airport.

Ernest Buehl announced the sale of the property, but at the same time he announced the opening of a new "Flying Dutchman" airfield. He had found a spot in nearby Bensalem and in 1954 opened the new airfield on the northeast corner of Hulmeville and Street Roads, where Brockwood Shopping Center now stands. Between 1955 and the early 1970s, Buehl continued teaching Northeast Philadelphians how to fly out of his Bensalem airport. Buehl lived until May 25, 1990, taking his last flight over his beloved Northeast Philadelphia only four years before he died.

The early interest in aviation from the people of Bustleton soon spread to surrounding communities. Experimentation with various forms of flight and efforts to improve the structures of airplanes marked aviation efforts in the 1930s and 1940s at other fields in Northeast Philadelphia. This led to the development and growth of the Boulevard and Budd Company airfields, both nearby. This in turn contributed to a land use pattern in the immediate area that now consisted of more landing field acreage than farm acreage.

Boulevard and Budd Airports Contribute to Aviation in the Northeast

If you happen to live in the area near Red Lion Road, Bustleton Avenue and Roosevelt Boulevard, chances are that your house or the local shopping center you frequent is located on the grounds of a former airport. From the late 1920s to the present, this section of Northeast Philadelphia would be home to four different airports. All have closed except the Northeast Airport at Grant Avenue and Academy Road. The sites of the other three are today taken up with housing developments and shopping centers, but from the 1920s to the 1990s they told the story of a different lifestyle in Northeast Philadelphia.

Besides the Bustleton airfield discussed in a previous section, there was the William Penn Airfield. It was begun in 1928 by Chester W. Larner, C.C. Tutwiler, H.W. Tutwiler and George R. Hutchinson, who formed a company to operate the airport on the site of the old Bustleton mail field. Located at Red Lion Avenue and Roosevelt Boulevard and operated by the Interstate Flying Corporation, the eighty-acre field had two runways and two hangars located next to the boulevard. It had six all-metal, modern-type planes available for daily use. There was a small restaurant across Red Lion Road that provided food and beverages for visitors. This building was recently torn down in 2008. In 1933, William Penn Airfield was purchased by Dick Bircher and renamed the Boulevard Airport. Beginning in 1937, it became known best as a testing site for early vertical takeoff convertiplanes. The planes were owned by Herrick Aircraft Company and designed by Gerald Herrick. His first gyrocopter, as he called it, was the Herrick HV-2A, which combined an innovative gyroplane rotor system with a conventional airplane.

George Townsend, a young and enthusiastic pilot from Northeast Philadelphia, flew Herrick's gyrocopter during its tests at Boulevard Airport.

Townsend made the first conversion from fixed wing to gyroplane in an April 1937 flight. By the end of the year, he had made one hundred conversions. On one flight, Townsend experienced such heavy vibrations after converting to gyroplane that he had to set down in someone's backyard on Academy Road, one block west of Frankford Avenue. After a few mechanical adjustments, Townsend took off again and remained in gyroplane mode for the flight back to Boulevard Airport.

By December 1937, Herrick's business was running out of money. The main problem was the instability of his gyrocopter's flight. Nearby aviator George Pitcairn in Bryn Athyn was having greater success developing what later became known as the helicopter. Pitcairn had purchased and developed the Willow Grove Airfield, where his experiments with gyrocopters were attracting investor interest. Pitcairn become the nation's leader in the field and by the 1950s had become a very rich man. Herrick, now out of money, was forced to abandon the HV-2A developmental program at the end of 1937.

In a rule that applied to all civil airports along the Atlantic coast during World War II, the Boulevard Airport was closed as a security measure by the U.S. government. However, in 1943 Gerald Herrick was given special permission by the government to experiment at the Boulevard Airport with his improved gyrocopter, the Herrick HV-3. Again he had little success with increasing the stability of the plane. His last attempt came in 1947, when he proposed a convertiplane with motor-mounted ramjets, but again neither the government nor investors were interested. Helicopter Engineering Research Corporation took over Boulevard Airport in 1951. The airport was closed to public use but reserved for test flights of the company's two helicopters, the Jovait-4E and the Javanovich JOV-3. This company also failed, forcing the sale of the airport to McCullick Motors Company in 1957. A 1958 aerial photo shows that houses were beginning to cover the western half of the former airport property. By 1970, the airport had disappeared from the map.

A third Northeast Philadelphia airport was built by the Edward G. Budd Company during World War II. Budd had been a major manufacturer of stainless steel railroad cars. Its initial entry into aeronautics was made in 1930 through a contract to make aircraft wheels and stainless steel wing ribs. In 1941, when the war broke out, the government requested that the company apply its manufacturing experience with stainless steel to building airplanes. The Budd Plant on Red Lion Road was enlarged and equipped by the government to produce new military planes. The first plane completed by Budd was the BB-1 Pioneer amphibian plane.

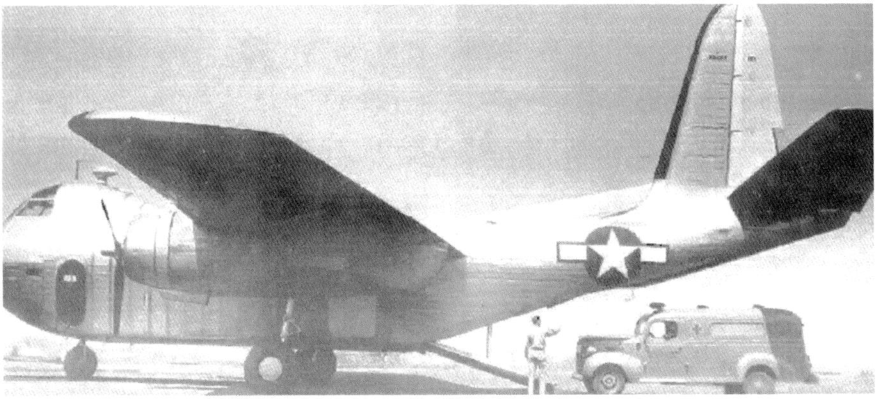

An aluminum airplane used to carry trucks was produced at the Budd Plant in 1941. The Budd RB-1 was manufactured at the Philadelphia Budd Plant as an experimental project to help the war effort. It was one of the first airplanes in the United States to have the structure to carry trucks.

New planes needed testing on a continuous basis, so Budd decided to build the region's first two totally concrete runways adjacent to the factory at Red Lion and Sandmeyer Lane, west of Roosevelt Boulevard. Budd's contribution to the war effort and flight was the use of stainless steel to build airplanes that were stronger and more durable. Its major project for the navy was the RB-1 Conestoga, a truck-carrying cargo transport designed by Gary Miller. In 1943, Budd built three prototypes, followed by a short production run of 17 planes for the navy. Local resident David Leidel was the test pilot for the RB-1 Conestoga. In all, there were well over a thousand Conestoga flights out of the Budd Airport. David Leidel's flight log still exists and chronicles daily mechanical breakdowns and near accidents while flying the Conestoga. These incidents led to the cancellation of the government contract for 180 RB-1 planes.

When the war ended, the twenty Conestoga planes already built were sold to the Flying Tiger Airline in China. The Budd Company then made the ill-fated decision to quit the airplane business and return to producing train cars. Its first big contract in 1955 to build "The Canadian" rail cars for the Toronto–Vancouver Railroad made the decision seem like a good one. By the 1960s, the company's former airfield was being used to store these rail car frames. Unfortunately, by the 1970s, the train industry fell into deep decline. Few trains were needed in an automobile-dominated society, and one contract could not carry a company as large as Budd. In April 1988, the last rail car rolled out of the Red Lion plant, and on the following Friday the last labor contract covering the workers expired. The Budd Company was sold in 1999 to Transit America Corporation. Transit America demolished the building and began selling off parts of the property. The land was sold to speculators and builders to be used for homes and shopping centers.

One last task remains to complete the story of aviation in Northeast Philadelphia. It is to explain the importance of the Northeast Chamber of Commerce campaign for its proposed Lincoln Airport in Northeast Philadelphia and the eventual development of Northeast Philadelphia Airport.

THE NORTHEAST PHILADELPHIA CHAMBER OF COMMERCE AND THE NORTHEAST PHILADELPHIA AIRPORT

In previous sections, we examined the history of the first airfields in Northeast Philadelphia. The Somerton and Boulevard airfields saw increased use in the 1930s with the growth of aviation in Northeast Philadelphia. It was a special weekend outing for many Philadelphia families to drive out Roosevelt Boulevard to see airplanes land and take off in Bustleton. This did not go unnoticed by the Northeast Philadelphia Chamber of Commerce, which saw the airports providing valuable transportation services to local industry. The chamber's newsletter, *The Nor'easter*—which the Historical Society of Frankford has copies of dating back to the founding of the organization in 1922—is filled with articles advocating a city-owned and city-supported Northeast Philadelphia Airport. It was the efforts of the chamber of commerce that would finally lead to a permanent airport in the Northeast.

From the beginning of the aviation industry, city officials had always favored a South Philadelphia location for the city's official airport. In the early 1930s, Pennsylvania had fewer than eighty airfields in operation, and there were only three or four within the city. The Hog Island field in South Philadelphia attracted most of the city's attention. To counter that preference, the Northeast Philadelphia Chamber of Commerce, led by Kern Dodge of Dodge Steel in Tacony, drew up a plan for a facility that would have all the necessities of a modern airport. Called the Lincoln Airport, it was to be located on the west side of Roosevelt Boulevard between Haldeman Street and Byberry Road (some motels in the area still bear the Lincoln name from this proposal). Dodge claimed that this airport could be put into service quickly and would cost the city far less than the Hog Island site. An important part of his plan was eliminating from city airports services for lighter-than-air ships. For Philadelphia and New York, this meant that landings by the *Graf Zeppelin*, blimps and balloons were to be stationed at Lakehurst, New Jersey, not at city airports.

Dodge's proposal was sent to Philadelphia City Council in 1933 but never adopted. City officials rejected the plan because of the hidden costs of a subway under Roosevelt Boulevard, road improvements and increased train transportation to the region that the Lincoln Airport would require. To council members, this was the Northeast Philadelphia Chamber of Commerce's way of procuring funds for city services in that section of the city, funds that the chamber felt the Northeast deserved but rarely got. Blocking the Lincoln Airport proposal were the Vare brothers of South Philadelphia, members of a politically powerful family in the city. They remained steadfast in favor of the Hog Island site since it meant jobs and increased industry for their constituents in South Philadelphia.

In 1937, Kern Dodge renewed his efforts to get approval from the city for the Lincoln airport. He invited world-famous aviator Colonel Clarence D. Chamberlain, who had flown nonstop from New York to Berlin in 1927 to speak on aviation before three hundred guests and city dignitaries at a Northeast Philadelphia Chamber of Commerce meeting at Evergreen Farms. This event prompted the chamber to again petition the city with an

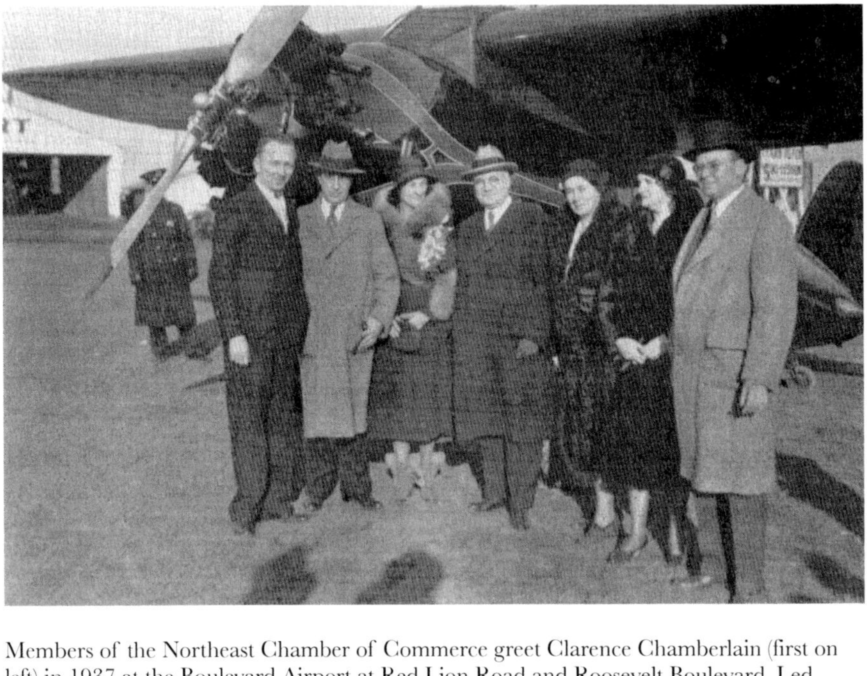

Members of the Northeast Chamber of Commerce greet Clarence Chamberlain (first on left) in 1937 at the Boulevard Airport at Red Lion Road and Roosevelt Boulevard. Led by Kern Dodge (center) and his wife, the chamber of commerce's meeting was aimed at making Northeast Philadelphia the location for the city's airport. Chamberlain was the second man to fly across the Atlantic. He did it two weeks after Lindberg, landing in Berlin in 1927.

amended proposal asking, "Which airport project should Philadelphia carry through?" The proposal then responded to its own question with, "Common sense dictates but one answer—BOTH, but the Northeast Airport should be FIRST because of its manifest economy and availability."

Finally, in 1939, the chamber's campaign for a city-owned airport in Northeast Philadelphia got a favorable reply from the city council. The city approved the purchase of 1,800 acres of land on the eastern side of the boulevard bounded by Grant Avenue and Academy Road for the construction of an airport with three runways. This was a clear rejection of the Lincoln Airport proposal, but the chamber was in favor of the plan since funding was forthcoming for the Northeast's first city airfield. The outbreak of World War II postponed work on the project by the city, but the United States Air Force took over the airfield during the war. The air force finished demolition of eighty-three homes to clear and level the site for runways. Pictures of every house removed from this location were taken in early 1945 and are now found in the collections of the Historical Society of Frankford. All houses were taken down, and in June 1945, the United

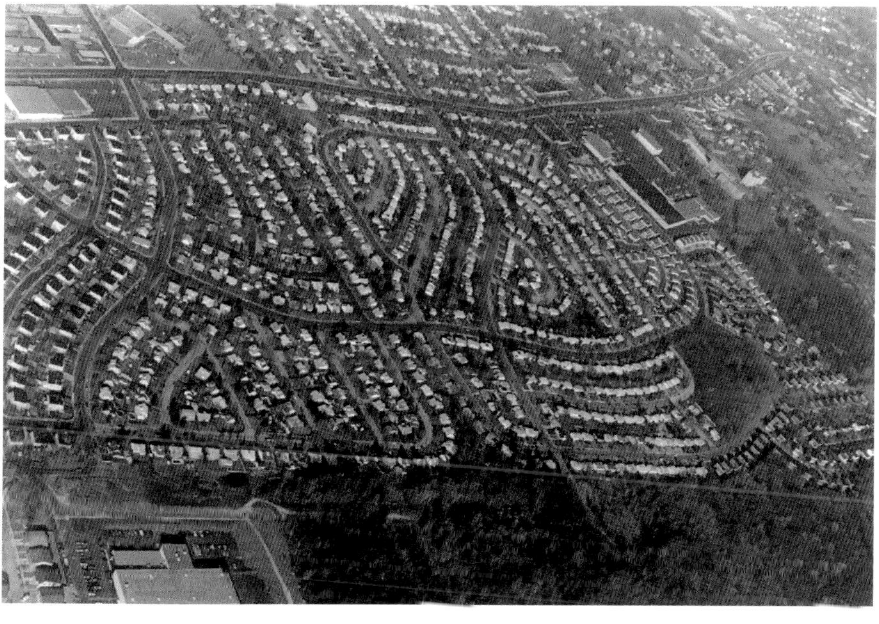

A 1965 view from the air of where the Flying Dutchman Airport used to be located. It has disappeared, replaced by circular housing patterns. Notice Bustleton Avenue at the top of the picture and the shopping center located in the upper right of the picture. The airports in the area led to a new type of building pattern for the Northeast. Rather than rectangular streets interconnecting, there were now circular patterns with streets that just seemed to end.

States government turned the facility over to the City of Philadelphia. The airport was officially named Northeast Philadelphia airport, and the Civil Aeronautics Administration took over the operation of the airport control tower at about the same time. The airport was growing in air traffic each year and becoming a modern airport.

While Northeast Philadelphia now had a city-owned airport, the idea of a large international airport in the Northeast began to fade in 1953. Philadelphia Airport at Hog Island was expanded and became Philadelphia's first international airport. The city now focused on the development of this airport and decreased funds for the Northeast Philadelphia Airport.

In the 1970s, the runways at Philadelphia International Airport were enlarged to seven thousand feet to accommodate large international jets. At the time, some Northeast businessmen advocated doing the same at Northeast Airport, but this suggestion led to protests from local homeowners near the airport. To them, the noise and air pollution was too large a cost to pay for allowing these flights at Northeast Airport. The city's reaction to the protests was to agree that Northeast Philadelphia Airport should remain limited to operating flight training schools, small plane flights and a small cargo service. It remains that way today.

In reviewing the history of aviation in Northeast Philadelphia, we can better understand our region's role in the development of aviation nationally. But how these aviation activities affected real estate development of the area is yet another story. The history of aviation in the Far Northeast goes a long way in explaining current housing patterns in the region. As we have seen, Bustleton and Somerton had four major airfields and one planned airfield (Lincoln Airport) set aside for development. This totaled over seven hundred acres of land that was in use up until 1954. No other section in the city had so much open ground in one cluster in the 1950s. Other communities in Northeast Philadelphia, like Mayfair, Oxford Circle, Burholme and Holmesburg, developed by continuing street patterns that were established in the early part of the century. Street names like Unruh, Walker, Knorr, Algon and Charles were just extended into open areas as these areas were developed. But such block patterns with continuous street names and numbering could not be used in much of the Far Northeast.

As blocks of land that were previously airfields were sold off in Bustleton and Somerton, the builders set aside large lots on Bustleton Avenue and Roosevelt Boulevard for shopping centers, and off from these major roads were set aside interior tracts for residential housing. This made economic sense, since commercial lots were far more profitable than residential lots. The residential tracts were formed into circular patterns with one or two entrance

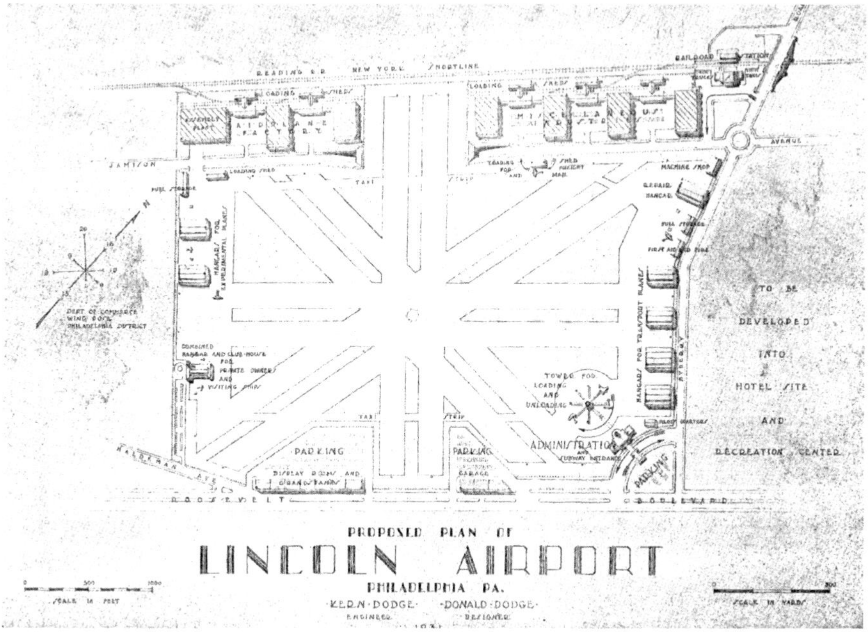

A drawing of the proposed Lincoln Airport, designed by Kern Dodge of the Northeast Chamber of Commerce in 1931.

streets per section. This became the accepted house pattern for the region so that when housing developments extended to Byberry, similar housing patterns were used. Contemporary aerial views of these sections show the distinctive patterns based on the location of the earlier airports. The two original roads, Roosevelt Boulevard and Bustleton Avenue, remain the area's main highways, while houses are located in developments with winding roads and circular street patterns. For those trying to locate a house in this section of the city, it can be a daunting task. No squared-off, continuous numbering system, no streets running in parallel rows. The history of airfields in Bustleton and Somerton best explains these unique housing patterns and makes these neighborhoods different from the rest of Northeast Philadelphia.

ROBERT PURVIS: BYBERRY ABOLITIONIST, 1810–1898

Prior to the Civil War, Byberry was home to one of America's most active and important abolitionists, Robert Purvis. Purvis's farm near Byberry Friends Meeting was the location for abolitionist meetings, the underground railroad and woman's rights activities.

Robert Purvis's father William, a white man and a native of England, made his fortune trading cotton in Charleston, South Carolina. His mother, Harriet Judah, was a born-free Negro. Robert was born August 4, 1810, in Charleston. Prejudice in Charleston dictated a move to the North, and the family settled in Philadelphia in 1819. Plans for sailing to England with their three sons ended with William's death in 1826. Soon after her husband's death, Harriet married William Miller, an African cleric from New York. The Purvis brothers inherited the wealth that their father had accumulated in Charleston. Robert and his brother Joseph liked Philadelphia and were left to grow up with James Forten, a charismatic African American business leader and abolitionist. They were treated like members of the family and both would eventually marry Forten daughters.

On James Forten's advice, Robert Purvis attended Amherst College in Massachusetts, and through his association with New England abolitionists, he became committed at the age of twenty to the antislavery cause. He contributed to the launching of William Lloyd Garrison's abolitionist newspaper, the *Liberator*; helped form the American Anti-Slavery Society; was

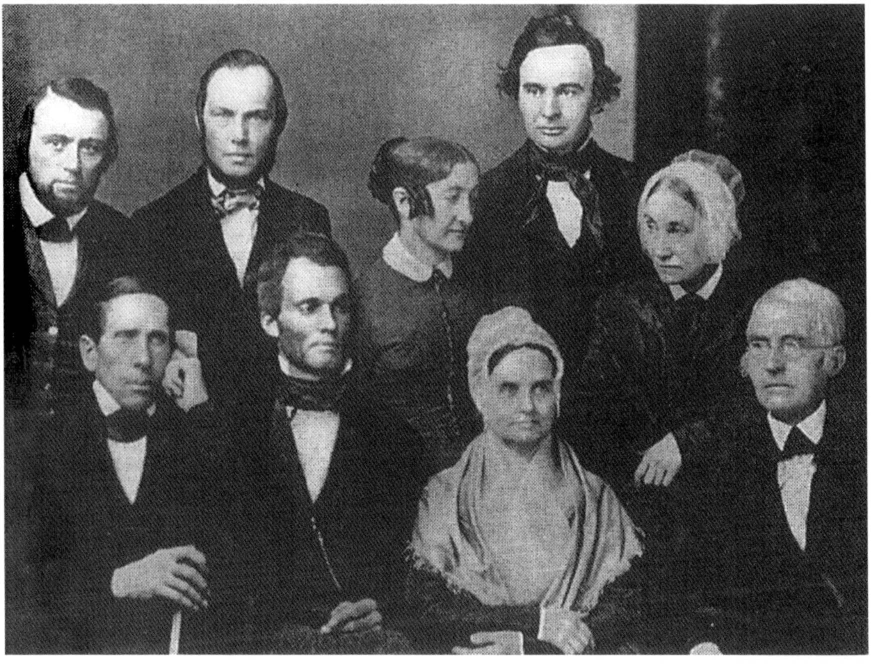

The Pennsylvania Anti-Slavery Society. President Robert Purvis is seated at center. To his left are Quaker abolitionists Lucretia Mott and James Mott. Members of this group were constant visitors to Purvis's farm.

known in Philadelphia as president of the underground railroad; founded the Pennsylvania Anti-Slavery Society; was active in the Moral Reform Society; and traveled to England during that country's debate over slavery.

Robert's brother Joseph did not become active in the antislavery movement. He married Sarah Forten and bought a farm in Bensalem, Bucks County, Pennsylvania. Beginning in 1835, he and Sarah devoted themselves to their Eddington Farm, making it a very successful enterprise that was admired by other farmers of the area.

About the same time, Robert Purvis married Harriet Forten, making James Forten a happy man. Robert had become like a son to Forten as they worked on antislavery causes in Philadelphia. In the summer of 1842, Robert Purvis, his wife and their abolitionist colleagues organized a temperance march and a celebration of the anniversary of the emancipation of African Americans in the British Empire. When the black marchers paraded next to the Irish neighborhood at Seventh and Bainbridge Streets, rocks were thrown from the crowd. The disruptions of the parade were traumatic for organizers Robert and Harriet Purvis. They were told that their home had been marked for attack. That night Robert took his wife and three children to his brother Joseph's house in Bensalem. He returned to Philadelphia the next day to protect his property. In the two days that followed, a full-scale riot broke out as mobs of whites burned black homes and churches. Purvis sat inside his front door with a rifle across his knee, waiting for the mob to

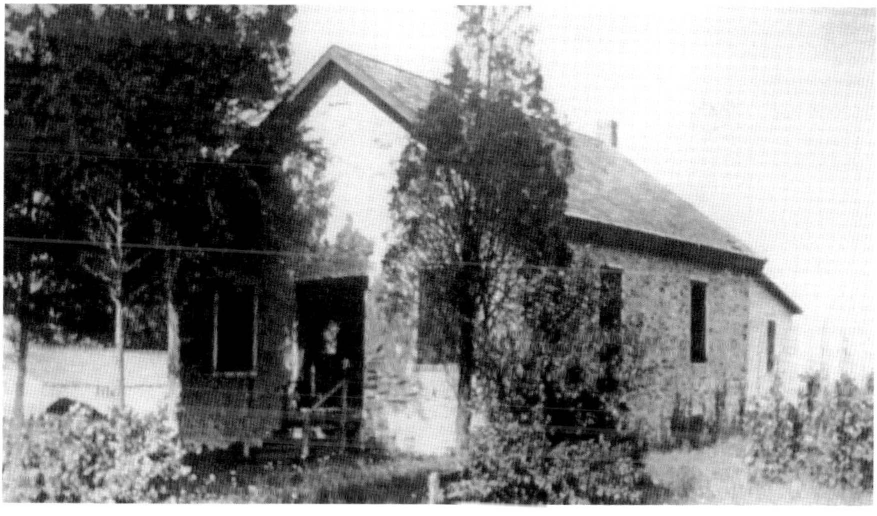

Byberry Hall was built by Robert Purvis in 1846 for antislavery meetings. It stands today east of the Byberry Quaker Meeting House.

enter his house. The mob came, loudly shouting his name, but a large fire in the next block distracted them. The mob gathered again the next day but was dissuaded from attacking the Purvis home by a local Catholic priest, Father Patrick Moriarty. When Sheriff Lewis Morris visited Purvis the next day and told him that he could no longer guarantee his safety in the city, Purvis immediately sold the house and went to live with his brother Joseph.

In 1843, Robert Purvis purchased a 104-acre farm in Byberry Township adjacent to the Byberry Friends Meeting House. This remained the family home for the next thirty years. Purvis had no difficulty in purchasing such a large estate because he had derived the major portion of his income from investments in real estate. He and his wife raised eight children on their farm. The most recognized of their children by the people of Byberry was their daughter Hattie. Hattie never married and lived most of her life there. Hattie knew the Quakers in the nearby meetinghouse, the many abolitionists who lived on nearby farms and the many prominent visitors to the Purvis house. She also knew Nancy Heaton of Byberry, who in 1848 was the first tavern keeper in Philadelphia County to adopt a prohibition against drinking. In later years, Hattie escorted one of the visitors at her house, Susan B. Anthony, to England.

Purvis proved to be a good neighbor. In 1846, he built Byberry Hall at his own expense to be used by the community and for antislavery meetings. In 1854, Purvis conveyed the Byberry Hall property in trust to his neighbors Emmor Comly, James Thornton and Joshua Newbold. Later Purvis sold the Quaker Meeting one acre of land for $200 to be used as a graveyard. Called the "new graveyard," it is still in use today.

Farming proved a great help for Robert in pursuing his antislavery agenda. A trip to the city with farm produce usually resulted in a return trip with a straw-covered wagon hiding runaway slaves. Robert kept meticulous records of the hundreds of slaves he helped escape, but with passage of the Fugitive Slave Law fear for his family's safety moved him to destroy these records.

The Purvis farm thrived in the mid-nineteenth century. The main emphasis was on cereal production and dairying, but they also sold meat and apples to the Philadelphia market. Harriet was as interested in farming as Robert and was a good judge of horses. The Purvises were especially interested in competing in local fairs in animal husbandry and selective breeding. Their participation was not always welcomed by some of their Byberry neighbors, however. Harriet and Robert had learned long ago that wealth could not shield them from racism. In 1846, there was a move to expel Robert from the Bensalem Horse Race Company, a local association of livestock breeders, on the basis of race. A few years later, after winning a string of prizes for his

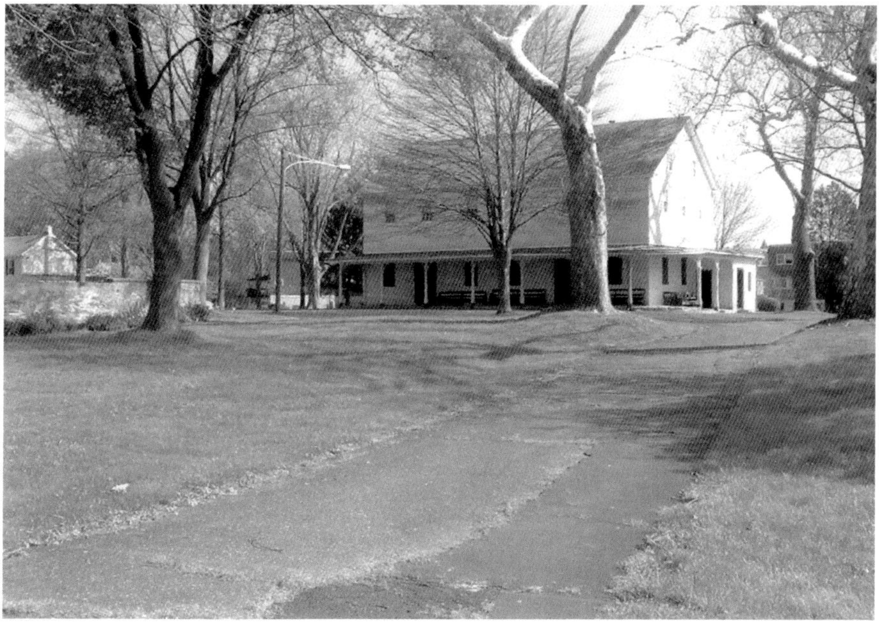

Byberry Friends Meeting House as it appears today.

poultry at the agricultural fair, he was told that black people could no longer show their birds.

In their Byberry home, Harriet and Robert entertained abolitionists and reformers from throughout the United States and abroad. Harriet was a gracious hostess. A cultured woman, she enjoyed music and arts. She was well read and refined and took pleasure in discussing the novels of the Brontë sisters and the poetry of Byron. On numerous occasions she entertained the families of William L. Garrison, Lucretia Mott, Susan B. Anthony and Wendell Phillips. She also fed and housed guests whose presence she carefully kept a secret. As they had done in their Philadelphia house, she and Robert had a special room constructed at Byberry to accommodate runaway slaves.

In 1847 and 1854, Purvis battled the local school board to allow his children to enter local schools. The Purvises paid the second-highest school tax in Byberry only to find their children barred from the local schools and forced to attend a "miserable shanty" in the nearby village of Mechanicsville. The Purvises preferred to educate their children at home and threatened to withhold school taxes. No record exists that this actually happened, however.

During the Civil War, the Purvises threw their energies into helping to free slaves. Harriet continued working with the Philadelphia Female Anti-

Slavery Society, organizing fairs and raising funds to assist freedmen and freedwomen. Robert worked at recruiting black troops for the Union army. In September 1863, as aide-de-camp to Major Stearns of the recruiting service of the army, Purvis worked at Camp William Penn in Cheltenham, representing the African American community of Philadelphia.

After the war, Harriet remained active in the feminist movement while Robert became active in getting the vote for blacks in Pennsylvania. Harriet became ill in the 1870s, and Robert stayed near her to comfort her. Despite his love and concern, Harriet died June 11, 1875, in Byberry. On March 5, 1878, Robert married Tacie Townsend, a white abolitionist seventeen years his junior, in a Quaker ceremony in Bristol, Pennsylvania, on March 5, 1878. Her father had been a neighbor of the Purvises in Byberry, and the two families had been friends for years. Tacie was a favorite of the Purvis children; they and the family responded well to the marriage. The marriage and the fact that his children were grown and had left home led Robert Purvis to sell the farm and leave Byberry. In 1878, he and his wife moved to Mount Vernon Street in North Philadelphia. It was there that he died of a stroke, with his wife Tacie at his side, April 15, 1898.

Part V
Torresdale

Camp Happy: A Children's Camp to Promote Health, 1921–1951

Few people living in Torresdale today remember the days when it was recognized throughout the country as having one of the nation's most successful social and health programs for children. Originating from the ideas of Jane Addams, founder of Hull House in Chicago, settlement houses soon spread to Philadelphia. Their purpose was to help the poor by improving their living standards and enabling children to receive proper food and healthcare. The influenza epidemic of 1918 spurred an increase in health concerns in the city. Thirteen thousand people had died in Philadelphia from influenza during September, October and November in 1918, with many corpses left in the streets. The board of health was overwhelmed and unable to meet the emergency. In the aftermath of this calamity, new laws were adopted that reverted back to the tried-and-true methods of improving health—fresh air, sunshine and exercise, especially for children.

In 1919, a new law was proposed to establish a Philadelphia Department of Recreation as part of the Welfare Department to provide playgrounds and activities for children throughout the city. The bill was specifically aimed at establishing play areas for children, and there was a special provision creating a children's summer camp. Called Camp Happy, it was to provide healthcare, dental care and proper nutrition, as well as recreational activities for Philadelphia's poor children.

Several locations were considered in the search for a site for the camp. Eventually a large tract of land on the southwest corner of Linden and

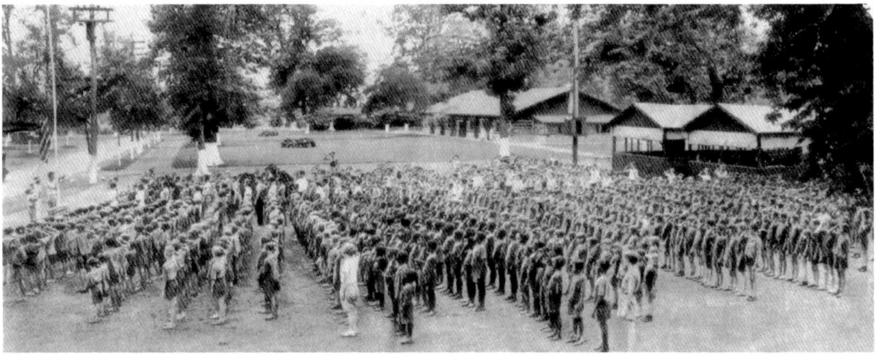

The morning flag salute on the parade grounds of Camp Happy in the summer of 1925.

Torresdale Avenues in Torresdale was chosen. Located in a large city-owned tract of land near the Delaware River, it seemed the ideal location. Fresh air, clean water, swimming facilities on the Delaware River at Point Pleasant and the state fish hatcheries nearby would provide opportunities for a variety of activities at the camp. The fish hatcheries were very popular with children. Torresdale hatcheries produced fifty-four million perch, Susquehanna salmon and frogs for state streams and rivers each year. All were grown from eggs transported to the hatcheries and placed in the various ponds surrounding the main building. Given all of these favorable conditions for a summer camp, the only thing necessary to open Camp Happy was a large dining hall (later called Kendrick Hall) and tents for overnight sleeping. City officials, armed with a predicted low cost for operating the camp, opened Camp Happy in the summer of 1920.

By 1925, the camp was accepting 1,800 boys and girls for the summer. The city had built twenty cabins, an activities hall, two swimming pools, a playground and baseball fields. The camp also included dentist and doctors offices and a counselors' cabin. The camp was often described as being founded for "tuberculosis-contact children." This meant that the children's environment had been tainted by tuberculosis, although they themselves had thus far escaped it. All of the children were considered undernourished and underweight. The camp population was made up of children from the families of Russian Jews, African Americans and Polish, with a small number of Irish and Germans.

The children, all between the ages of seven and twelve, were selected by nurses assigned to the free clinics run by the Philadelphia Department of Public Health. They were taken to the camp in buses. Upon arrival, they were issued khaki shorts and shirts to be worn at the camp. Their personal

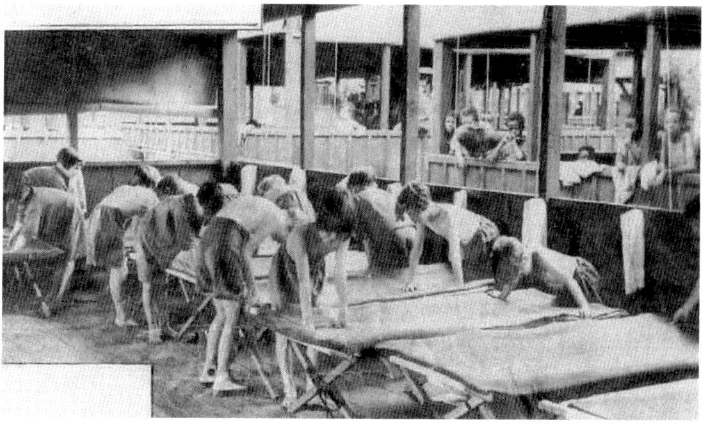

Cabins were kept clean and neat. Pictured here is a group getting ready for inspection.

clothes were stored until their encampment was over. Sixty counselors were placed in charge of all activities. Many of these were volunteers from local colleges who received free room and board for the summer. There were swimming contests, games, music and visits to the fish hatcheries and Point Pleasant Beach for boat rides on the Delaware. In arts and craft sessions, the boys were taught to work in leather and metals, while the girls learned to sew and embroider.

For three weeks, these children were to experience the healthiest form of living. The camp had two swimming pools (both with new chlorinators) sliding boards, swings, a merry-go-round, sandboxes and a baseball diamond. Fresh air, special diet, proper activities, health exams and rest systematically were included in the daily schedule. Also on the schedule were three planned meals a day and four milk breaks. The brushing of teeth after each meal was mandated, and exercise through games and activities were planned.

There were no chores for the children except the obligation to make their beds and keep the cabins clean. Cleanliness was rewarded with a lollypop, which many of the children saved to take home to a younger brother or sister. During rest periods in the cabin, counselors often read stories to the children.

Two graduate nurses and a doctor were on duty at all times. A dentist examined each child for tooth decay. By the time the children went home, their cavities had all been corrected. In health reports at the end of each year, the medical staff announced that "each child had an average gain of eight pounds in weight."

Once a year the city officials sponsored "Mayor's Day" at the camp. It was a special day with lots of visitors, special treats for the children and much publicity for the politicians. Visits by Mayors Moore, Mackey, Wilson

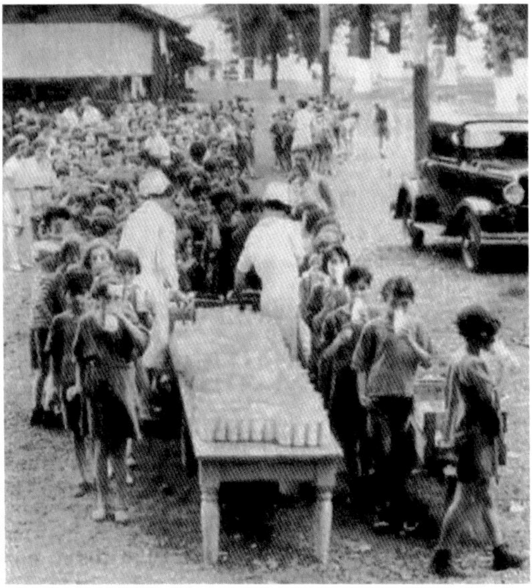

Children lined up four times a day for a glass of milk. Since all of the children in the camp were malnourished, milk was considered a necessity by city health officials.

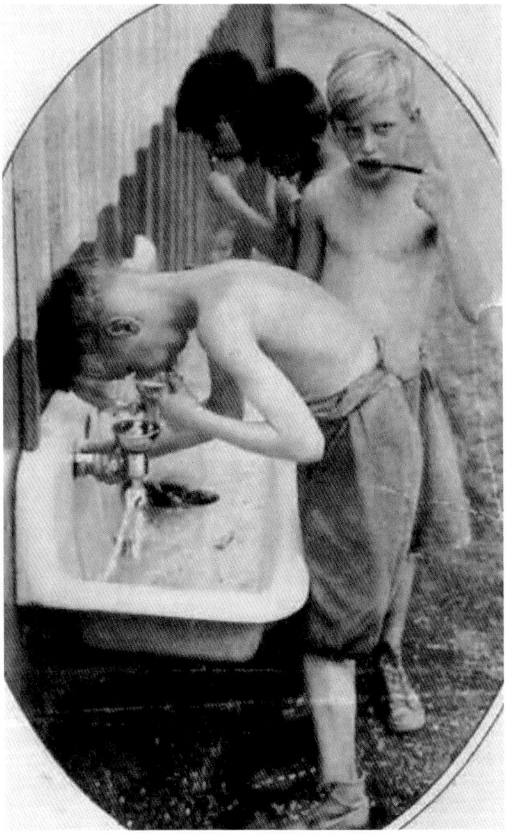

Children at Camp Happy were given toothbrushes and were required to brush their teeth twice a day.

and Samuel over the years were accompanied by vaudeville shows, games and prizes, capped off with party cake and ice cream for the campers. The mayors praised Camp Happy and the work being done to improve the health of the children of Philadelphia. The publicity generated by the Mayor's Days at Camp Happy was used to show the citizens of the city how the mayor helped the children of the city. During the Great Depression in the 1930s, Camp Happy continued as one of the city's premier programs aimed directly at the poor. Hikers and visitors to nearby Point Pleasant Beach were encouraged to stop and see the "inspiring" sight of the children at Camp Happy.

In the years following World War II, increased development in the Torresdale area and the pollution of the Delaware River made the location less desirable. Also, the new 1952 Home Rule Charter reorganized Camp Happy's board, placing it under the Department of Recreation, led by Robert Crawford. A recreation specialist more focused on camp experience than the health issues of children, Crawford purchased a summer camp in the Pocono Mountains from Girard College for $25,000. A contest was held by the last group of youngsters attending Camp Happy to rename the new camp in the Poconos. Camp William Penn was selected as the name of the new site, and Camp Happy closed in 1951. Because the land was owned by the Department of Recreation, much of the old site became a playground.

Glen Foerd, the Polish Population of Bridesburg and a New Industry for the Northeast

For those who have experienced the beauty and splendor of the Glen Foerd Mansion in Torresdale, there is a great appreciation for how the rich lived in Philadelphia in 1900. In Northeast Philadelphia, a wealthy industrialist such as Robert H. Foerderer could live a life of luxury on the banks of the Delaware River not far from his factory. But there is a deeper story behind the beautiful estates and lavish lifestyles: that of how wealthy industrialists influenced ethnic population trends and the growth of new industries in the city.

Foerderer acquired his mansion on the Delaware in 1893 and named it Glen Foerd, combining part of his own name with that of Glengarry, the name given to the estate by its former owner, Charles Macalester. Foerderer owned the most successful leather factory (known as VICI KID) in Philadelphia. It was located in Frankford at Wheatsheaf Lane and Arcadia Streets near Frankford Avenue and employed 1,500 workers at a time, mostly from the

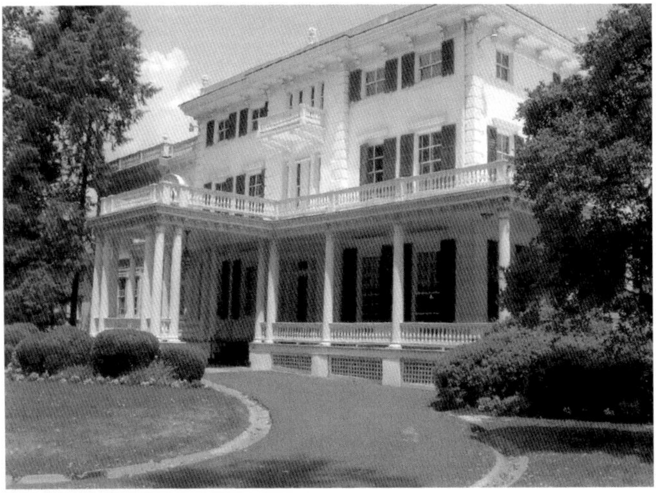

The main driveway leading to the front entrance of the Glen Foerd Mansion in Torresdale, 2008.

Polish populations of Port Richmond and Bridesburg. The factory produced leather from goat hides for shoes, handbags and belts. Foerderer spent much time at the factory but also took frequent trips around the world in search of better and cheaper leather hides. These trips enhanced the beauty of his home, since his second-floor art gallery housed paintings, artifacts and fur cases acquired in his travels.

The leather business then was dirty, smelly and exhausting work. Smells were a particular problem for workers since leather tanning at the Foerderer plant prior to 1909 entailed using milk of lime to remove the hair from the hide and then dipping it into a vat of dog dung or pigeon manure overnight. Placing one's hands in vats of lime and then dog dung was considered even then the worst of jobs. Few would accept working at the factory except the newly arrived Polish immigrants, whose only other option was work in the coal mining industry in the small towns of upstate Pennsylvania (again, work that few others would take). So it was that during the early twentieth century Bridesburg's population changed from mostly German to mostly Polish, primarily due to the hiring practices at the Foerderer Leather Works. The St. John Cantius Polish Catholic Church in Bridesburg soon became one of the largest Polish churches in Philadelphia. Despite their hardships, few Polish workers considered themselves abused or persecuted. They were hard workers, very religious and simply looking for a better life.

One such worker was Frank Sikorski, who left his home in an eastern province of Poland in 1905 to come to Philadelphia. In a recent interview with his son, Frank Sikorski Jr., a ninety-one-year-old former resident of Bridesburg who now lives in Mayfair, Frank Sr.'s life at Foerderer Leather

Works unfolds. From his friends in Poland, the older Sikorski knew of the Foerderer Leather Works and the Polish populations in Port Richmond and Bridesburg before he came to Philadelphia. Upon his arrival here, he could not speak a word of English; he knew only Polish and a little German. He stayed with a friend his first night in Port Richmond and went to Foerderer to seek work the next day. He was hired by a Polish supervisor to remove hair from the goat fur, using milk of lime and dung, one of dirtiest jobs in the factory. Sikorski never complained, and he worked hard every day, enduring the smell, the lime and the dog dung contact. The language barrier was no problem, since most of the workers spoke Polish and most of the bosses spoke German. Sikorski always had many German friends and felt that his knowledge of the German language helped him greatly in America.

After a few years of hard work and good attendance, Sikorski was promoted to the foremanship of a dozen workers who were responsible for trimming excess fat from the goat skins prior to hair removal. He married a Polish girl from Port Richmond in 1911, and his son Frank Sikorski Jr. was born a few years later. He also helped many other Poles get jobs at Foerderer Leather Works. As is true with most immigrant groups, the Poles had their own internal network for job seeking. When Frank Jr. reached fifteen years of age, he too became a worker at Foerderer, assigned directly under his father. His father had the respect of the men who worked under him, and he was known as a fair, honest man but a taskmaster not to be questioned.

Frank Sikorski, in his role as supervisor, actually knew Robert Foerderer's son Percival (1884–1969), who took over the works after his father's death in 1903. Not that they were friendly, but to be spoken to by the owner was a great honor. Frank Sr. often told his son of an encounter he had with Mr.

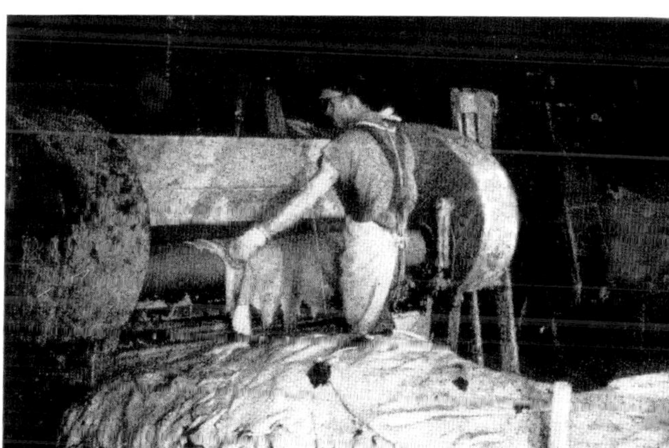

The Foerderer factory had ten of these hair-removal machines. After soaking in milk of lime and dung, the goat hair was removed by using this machine. Hides were then stretched and dried. Frank Sikorski and his father worked in this part of the shop for years.

Foerderer in 1930. Foerderer approached him at the factory to ask if he did any handyman work. Sikorski replied that he did, and Foerderer told him that he needed a group of men to remove a large gas chandelier at Glen Foerd. One day he arrived at work to be put in a truck with a few other men to be taken to the Glen Foerd estate on the Delaware. The mansion was beautiful, the air from the river pure and everything so clean. They were all given white gloves to wear while working in the house. Piece by piece the old chandelier was removed and boxed, and a new one was installed. It took a full day. No one minded, the work was not hard, they were given lunch and they were still receiving the same hourly pay they would have received at the factory. Activities such as this cemented the loyalty of supervisors like Frank Sikorski, who rarely had a bad word to say about the company.

Sikorski was a supervisor at Foerderer during a period of significant change in the leather-tanning process. Dr. Otto Rohm, a German scientist, had been working on an artificial substance to replace the dog dung used in the leather-softening process. In 1906, he invented Oropon, a synthetic material that could be used in place of the dung. Rohm and businessman Otto Haas organized the Rohm & Hass Company in Germany in 1907. Haas was given the responsibility of selling the new product. He researched leather manufacturers in the United States, looking for a large company he could approach with the new product. He decided on the Foerderer Leather Works in the Frankford section of Philadelphia. In 1909, Haas came to Philadelphia and signed a contract with Foerderer to provide Oropon for use in his factory. Next, Haas purchased a building in nearby Bridesburg to produce Oropon for customers in the United States. Rohm & Haas began as a small company, producing Oropon for leather manufacturers. At the beginning of World War II, the company invented Plexiglas, which could be used for making windshields for airplanes. At the same time, the leather trade was being decimated by new plastic substances that often replaced leather. Foerderer Leather Works would go out of business by the 1940s, while Rohm & Haas was destined to become one of the largest chemical manufacturers in the United States, providing Northeast Philadelphia with thousands of jobs. Most recently, Rohm & Haas was sold to Dow Chemical Company, the largest chemical company in the world.

As one looks at the beautiful Glen Foerd Mansion today, it should be remembered that the building is more than an impressive home from a previous time. It represents wealth garnered from the hard work of Polish immigrants, the settlement of a Polish community in Bridesburg and the establishment in Northeast Philadelphia of one of the largest chemical companies in the nation. This story also demonstrates that history is rarely one story, but a collection of events that often lead to unexpected outcomes.

PART VI

BURHOLME

BURHOLME: ONE OF THE OLDEST COMMUNITIES IN NORTHEAST PHILADELPHIA

One of the oldest communities in Northeast Philadelphia, although it is not generally recognized as such, is Burholme. As early as the 1770s, a quaint little village had developed at the junction of Township Line Road (Cottman Avenue), Second Street Pike (Rising Sun Avenue) and Oxford Pike. This crossroads became known as "Five Points." The most heavily traveled road of the three was Oxford Pike, which was a toll road to Frankford. Toll roads were very important to farmers because they could be relied upon for taking produce to market. We know that Oxford Pike was a success because its shareholders' return on an investment averaged 6 percent in the years 1800 and 1850. A typical country center in early America, Five Points had a wheelwright shop, a blacksmith, a carpenter and a grocery store. The old toll gate for the Oxford Pike stood at Rising Sun Avenue and Oxford Pike, with a second toll gate where Oxford Circle is on the boulevard, although the boulevard was not completed until after 1914.

That the Five Points community is an old community is borne out by the age of the two oldest churches in the area: the Ye Old Pennypack Baptist Church on Krewstown Road, founded in 1688, and the Trinity Church Oxford (Episcopal), founded in 1698 on Oxford Turnpike (Oxford Avenue). These dates provide some indication of how early the region was settled.

As late as 1889, Oxford Pike was the main route to Frankford, which represented the outside world to many residents of upper Northeast Philadelphia. Unfortunately, the spring rain often made the trip to Frankford

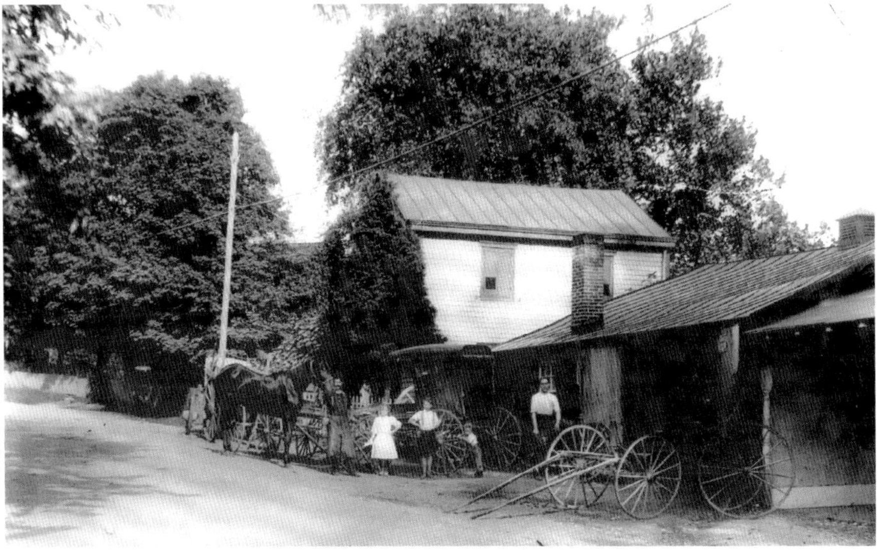

A typical old village smithy as found in the Five Points area in 1925.

impossible, and farm produce would pile up at the Five Points junction. Local farmers petitioned the toll road company to plank the surface of the road all the way to Frankford—a process that entailed laying one board after another to form a wooden road. This was done with the help of the farmers, and the plank road lasted until the company stoned the road five years later. Nevertheless, Five Points remained isolated for decades. Rising Sun Avenue was not completed to run to Burholme until 1899, when the No. 50 trolley line was opened, and Cottman Street remained a dirt road until 1929, when it was paved to serve as an east–west road to the Tacony-Palmyra Bridge.

A number of activities of the local residents in the nineteenth century attempted to put "Five Points" on the map. In the 1840s, a group of men interested in horse racing organized the Oxford Pike Racing Association. They rented land north of Rising Sun Avenue near Cottman Avenue and opened a racetrack for horses. Local farmers began to race their best horses at Five Points. However, the powerful Jeanes family opposed horse racing on the moral grounds that it promoted gambling. They purchased the land (which is Jeanes Hospital today) and closed down racing in the community forever.

A major political controversy in the community occurred in 1858, when a post office branch was opened in Kerper's grocery store (Kerper Street is named for the store) in Five Points after being moved from Hollowell's corner at Martin's Mill Road and Second Street Pike. Why was the post office

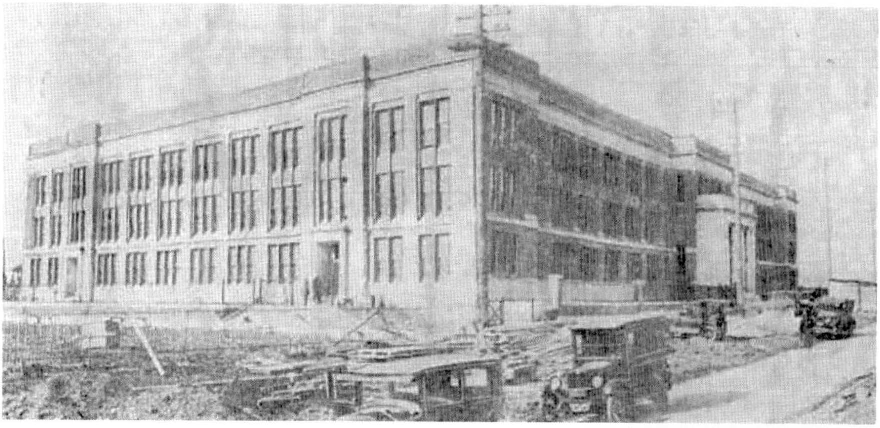

A picture of Cottman Avenue in 1928, showing the building of Woodrow Wilson Jr. High School near Five Points. As you can see, Cottman Avenue has only one small lane with few cars.

moved to such an isolated location? The people of Five Points had requested Edward Buchanan, pastor of Trinity Church Oxford and brother of U.S. president James Buchanan, to change its location to enhance the status of Five Points. This became one of the rare instances where a president of the United States intervened in a local dispute in Northeast Philadelphia. The post office remains in Burholme to this very day.

The area around Five Points has always had a reputation for being very patriotic. That reputation was initiated by its experience in the Civil War. When the Civil War began in 1861, community leader Captain W. Garry called for volunteers to fight the Rebels. He mustered the men in formation at Township Line Road and Oxford Pike, now Cottman and Oxford Avenues. Spectators watched as the company, which was to represent Five Points in the Civil War, was sworn in. Garry told the men, gathered relatives and friends that "today we are going south to fight the enemy. If there is a man among you who doesn't want to go and fight, step out and go home." They all stayed and went to war. Sadly, of the 103 men lined up that day, only three were alive at the end of the war. By 1876, only one, Harry Stanwood, was alive and well living in Frankford. No other section of Northeast Philadelphia suffered the losses experienced by Five Points in the Civil War.

Outstanding among the residents of Five Points was Robert Waln Ryerss, who built his summer home and moved into the area in 1859. He named his home Burholme in honor of his ancestral home in England. After Ryerss's death, in accordance with the terms of his will, the property was given to the City of Philadelphia to be used as a park. Once the Ryerss estate became city property, the residents of Five Points voted to change the name of the community to Burholme as a way of showing appreciation to Ryerss for his gift of a park for the community. The beautiful mansion became a museum and library in 1910, and the seventy acres of rolling lawns and gardens were to always be open to the public. Today, in what has become perhaps the biggest controversy in the history of Burholme, Fox Chase Cancer Center plans to use part of this land to expand its facilities.

As we have described, Burholme was for many years a farming community connected to the Frankford produce and merchandise market by Oxford Pike. That would all change in 1899, when the No. 50 trolley line was finished to Burholme. This allowed skilled workers and tradesman from elsewhere in the city to migrate up Rising Sun Avenue into the Northeast. First settled was Cresentville, with many workers getting jobs at the Crescent Rope factory, followed later by the development of the Lawndale Land Company. Mostly settled by Germans, Lawndale consisted of single or twin homes, offering an openness that did not exist in the older neighborhoods of the city. In the 1950s, the small village of Marburg at Comly Street and Robbins Avenue filled the gap between Lawndale and Burholme. Since the No. 50 trolley went directly through the German immigrant enclave near Fifth and Girard Avenues, many Germans bought the homes on Rising Sun Avenue in Lawndale and Marburg. This new route for migration into the area accelerated the change from a farming region to a residential neighborhood.

As the population increased, there was a need for improvements in schools, roads, lighting and sewers. In 1910, the Burholme Improvement Association was organized to work toward these improved standards of living. In 1928, the association was able to convince the Philadelphia School Board to build the Wilson Jr. High School on Cottman Avenue just north of Castor Avenue, the first secondary school to be built north of Frankford. By the 1930s, the association, working closely with Clarence K. Crossan, a city councilman who lived in Burholme, got ten new streets paved, with water and sewer lines adjacent to the Five Points location. In 1937, the Pennsylvania state legislation's Ten Year Payment Bill provided a means of paying for sewers over an extended period of time, which allowed most of the houses in the community to get modern water and sewage services. Also, in the same decade, the first recreation center was opened in Burholme in a renovated old house. From its origins as an early crossroads in the colonial period, Burholme had become a vibrant residential community.

Part VII

General Northeast Area

Al Schmid: Reluctant World War II Hero

One of the most famous heroes of World War II was a native of Northeast Philadelphia. Albert Schmid gained national recognition for his exploits in the Battle of Guadalcanal, killing two hundred Japanese soldiers during a five-hour attack, many after he had been blinded by a hand grenade. The wounds resulted in the removal of one eye and blindness in the other. Presented with the Navy Cross in February 1943, Schmid became a national hero. In Philadelphia, a parade was given in his honor, and the *Philadelphia Inquirer* presented him with its Hero Award and $1,000. In New Orleans, Schmid received the keys to the city. Articles appeared in *Life* and *Cosmopolitan* magazines describing his bravery on Guadalcanal. Author Roger Butterfield wrote Schmid's story in book form, entitled *Al Schmid, Marine*, and in 1944 Warner Brothers Studio purchased rights to the book. A year later the nation was treated to the movie *Pride of the Marines*, featuring John Garfield and Eleanor Parker.

The movie was an instant hit—not because of its combat scenes, which comprised only ten minutes of the film, but because of the dogged determination shown by his fiancée Ruth Hartly to help Schmid return to a normal life. People responded to this moving, honest portrayal of Schmid's recuperation and efforts to adjust to life as a visually impaired man. Ruth's love and willingness to accept the man she had pledged to marry despite what the war had done to him was an inspiration to many Americans.

Born in 1920, Schmid was a typical boy from Northeast Philadelphia in the 1930s and '40s. Raised in Burholme from the time he was two years old,

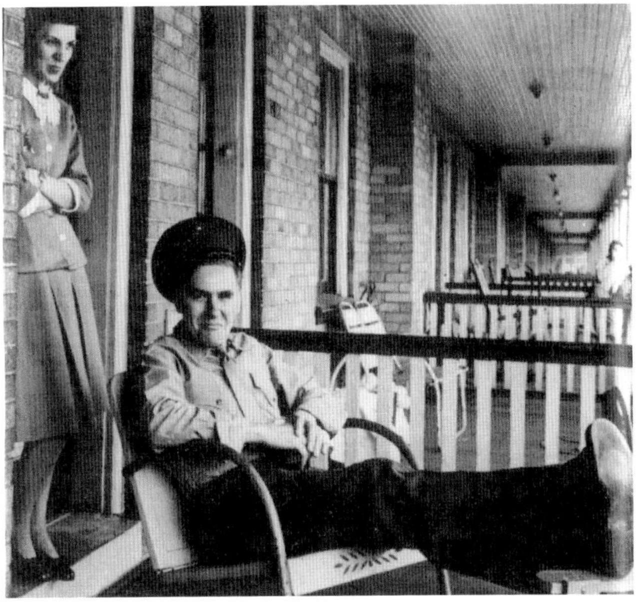

Al Schmid sitting on the front porch of Jim Merchant's house on the 6500 block of Tulip Street in Tacony. Al rented the back bedroom for the two years he worked at the Dodge Steel Company at McGee Street and State Road. Ruth Hartley stands in the doorway.

he considered Five Points, the World War I Memorial and Oxford Avenue to be his home turf. His mother died when he was ten years old, and he was left to grow up with his father. This made him independent at an early age. Schmid loved to hunt birds, rabbits and mice with his BB gun in the open farm areas near his home. He was a good student in school, majoring in mechanical drawing at Wilson Junior High School. He was also the class clown, preferring a good laugh over a good grade. For one of his pranks, he left a box with a snake in it on the teacher's desk just to see her get startled. No one in the class would tell on him, so the whole class remained after school for punishment. At one point, he left school to go to work on a farm in Lancaster County. Schmid was a good worker, often doing the work of two men. The farm job lasted a year, after which he moved back with his father.

In 1940, he heard of an opening for a job as an apprentice burner at the Dodge Steel Company at State Road and Magee Street in Tacony. Since he could not afford his own place, Schmid lived with fellow worker Jim Merchant and his wife Ella Mae in a row home at 6508 Tulip Street. It was here that he met Ruth Hartley, a close friend of Ella Mae's. They dated continually in the year before the war.

Nine days after Pearl Harbor, Schmid enlisted in the U.S. Marines and went off to Parris Island, South Carolina, for training. Before leaving for active duty in the Pacific, he asked Ruth to marry him, giving her a wedding ring purchased with a sixty-dollar bonus check that he had gotten from Dodge Steel.

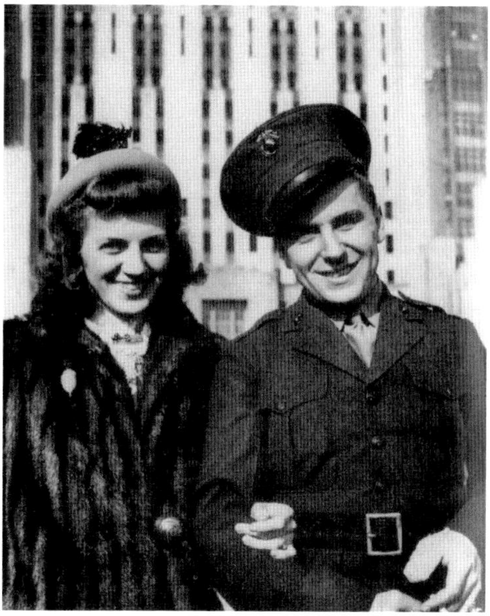

Al Schmid returns home in 1942 after being wounded in battle. Notice the bandaged thumb from an injury suffered at Guadalcanal in 1941, where he was also blinded by a grenade. This picture of Al Schmid and Ruth Hartley was taken when he returned to Philadelphia after hospitalization in San Diego.

She was a Frankford girl who lived with her aunt at 1025 Filmore Street. Much of Ruth and Al's time before the war was spent in Frankford and Tacony. Schmid always considered himself a Frankford boy, going back to the days when he courted Ruth. They attended movies at the Liberty movie house on Torresdale Avenue and picnicked in Pennypack Park. The last movie they saw together before he left was *Sergeant York* with Gary Cooper. Ruth remembered how Al commented that he would kill more of the enemy than York did in the movie.

After his injury at Guadalcanal, Schmid's shrapnel wounds and eye injuries were treated in a San Diego army hospital in 1942. It was then that he wrote to Ruth that he had lost one eye and had no sight in the other. He wrote, "I don't want to be a burden to you" and said he would understand if she wanted to move on with her life. Ruth refused to move on without him, telling her friend Edna Dietrich, "I can't let him go because I love him too much." Eventually, she convinced him of her love, and they were married in April 1943. This prompted Warner Brothers to consider calling the movie about Schmid *This Love of Ours*, but war movies seemed to be selling better than love stories in 1944, so they called it *Pride of the Marines*. Moving to Vista Street east of Frankford Avenue in Mayfair after their wedding, the couple had their first and only child in 1944, Al Schmid Jr.

Schmid's life in Philadelphia after the war is well remembered by Ted Bohn of Mayfair. He had met Schmid through his uncle, who hung out with

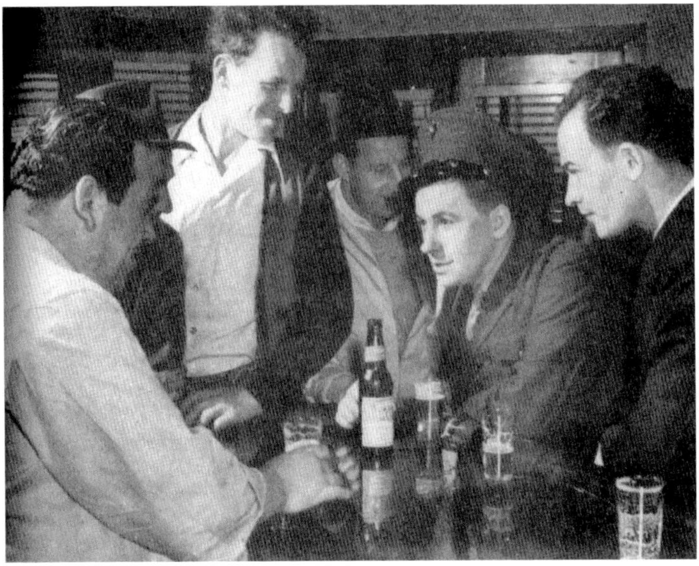

Al Schmid and his buddies meet at Al Henninger's taproom in Tacony. Al loved to spend time with his old buddies from Tacony.

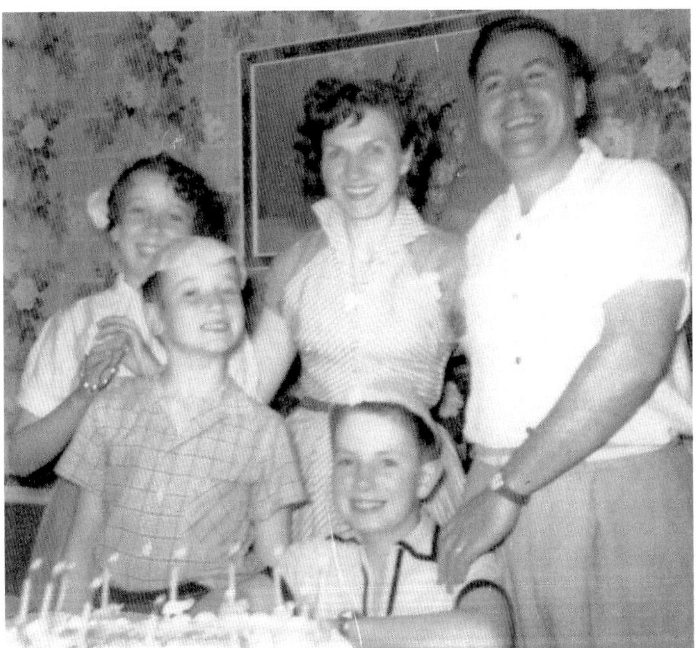

A happy Al Schmid and his wife Ruth Hartley at the birthday party of Al Schmid Jr. It was the 1950s, when the family lived on Vista Street in Mayfair.

"the gang" at Frankford American Legion Post 211 at Lieper and Overington Streets. Bohn remembered what a thrill it was to first meet Schmid, who told him "don't ever call me a hero." Schmid believed that the real heroes were the men who gave their lives "over there." Driven by his friends or his wife, Al would go to Frankford Post 211 almost daily to hang out with his buddies. They talked about the gophers (the nickname for marines on Guadalcanal) and about John Garfield, who had lived with Schmid for a short while so he could imitate his blindness for the movie. Al often recounted the story of the crowds of people that came to Tulip Street in Tacony and Fillmore Street in Frankford to see the shooting of scenes for the movie.

One of the tricks played on strangers at Post 211 concerned Schmid's ability to count paper money. His wife would fold each denomination differently so that Al knew how much money he had. He would place the money on the bar knowing exactly each denominations' pile. Once, a stranger became fascinated by Al's ability to pay his bill without help. He asked him, "How do you do that?" Al responded, "I feel the money." Being a little of a smart aleck, the stranger took out a ten-dollar bill, gave it to Al and asked, "How

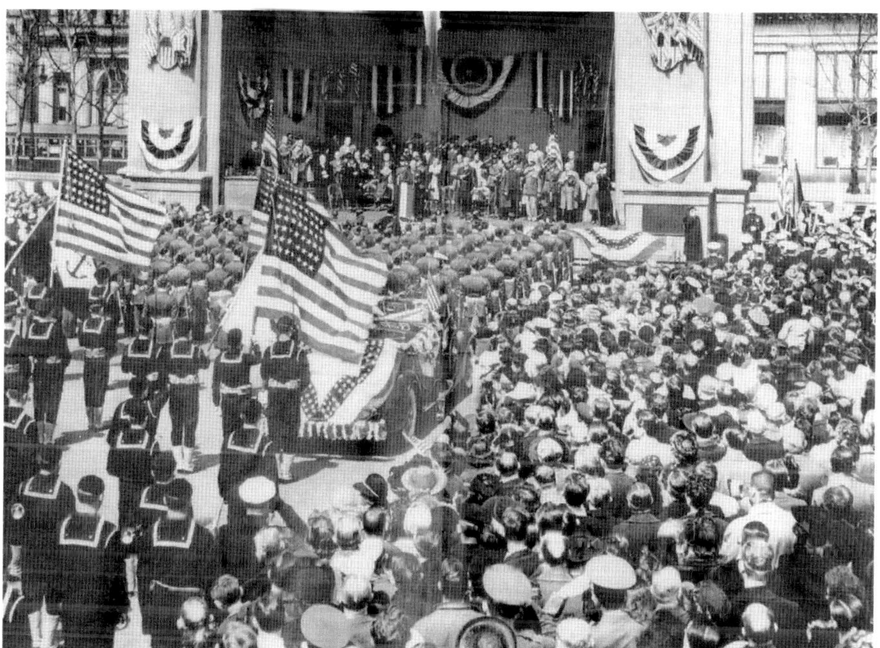

Al Schmid is honored by the City of Philadelphia as a war hero at Rayburn Plaza in 1943. A motion picture of his life followed, called *Pride of the Marines*. It starred John Garfield and Eleanor Parker.

much is this?" Al began feeling the bill. One of his buddies, Bill Bradley, a World War I vet, seeing what was happening, went to the bar and tapped Schmid ten times, an act unnoticed by the stranger. Al then announced to all that it was a ten-dollar bill. The stranger left befuddled, and Al's Post buddies were ecstatic. A good joke was still the most fun in Al's life.

By 1957, the cold winters had begun to affect Al's health. His glass eye would freeze to the eye socket, endangering the tissue behind the eye. Staying indoors was not a solution. Doctors recommended that the family move to Florida near the Bay Pines Veterans Hospital in St. Petersburg, which they did. In Florida, Al learned to enjoy fishing and became a ham radio operator. His happiness was short-lived, however, when in 1962 his eighteen-year-old son was killed in an automobile accident coming home from a military school he was attending. Edna Dietrich remembers well Ruth's call from Florida telling her old friend about her son's death and her husband's despondency. Ruth and Al lived on in Florida until Al's death on December 2, 1982, in St. Petersburg. He was buried with full military honors in Arlington National Cemetery in Washington, D.C., recognized as one of America's heroes of World War II.

THE FIRST AIRPLANE FLIGHT SEEN IN NORTHEAST PHILADELPHIA, 1910

One of the most exciting events in Northeast Philadelphia history was the first flight through the area in 1910. The history of flight in America begins with the Wright brothers in Kitty Hawk, North Carolina, in 1903, and the first powered, controlled flight by man. More perfected flight required another fifteen months of practice in Dayton, Ohio, but by 1905 the Wrights were ready to demonstrate to the world their ability to fly. The proof to most Americans occurred on October 4, 1909, when Wilbur made his now-famous flight above the Hudson River from the Statue of Liberty to West Point in New York. One million spectators lined the banks of the river to witness the flight, and the nation's newspapers headlined the events of the day, signaling the onset of the age of flight in America. The excitement caused by Wilbur's flight also appealed to entrepreneurs, who saw that big money could be made from air shows. So it was that 1910 became the year for air shows, races and stunts, starting with the famous January air show in Los Angeles. The Wright brothers had three crews at that event. The only foreign entrant was Louis Paulhan, of France, who brought two Farman biplanes from France. These biplanes were to become involved in Northeast Philadelphia's introduction to manned flights.

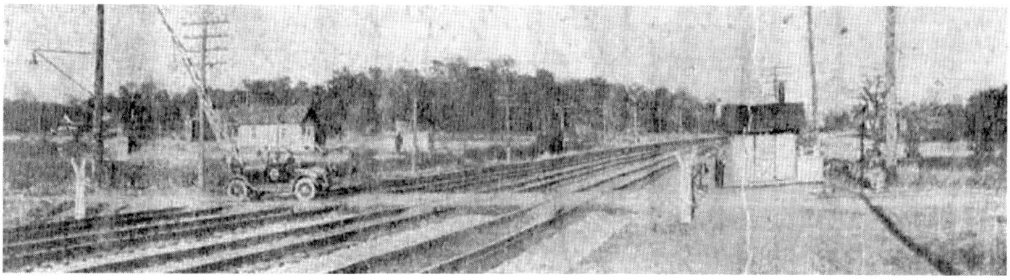

The railroad crossing at Linden Avenue and the Pennsylvania Railroad in 1920. There were over five hundred people from the Northeast there on June 13, 1910, to see their first airplane flight.

The first flight in the city of Philadelphia was arranged in June 1910 by the *Philadelphia Public Ledger* and the *New York Times*, both of which funded the event. Its purpose was to demonstrate that it was possible for a plane to fly from New York to Philadelphia, land, take off and return the same day. If completed, the flight would set a world record for nonstop distance by a plane. Newspapers carried the story of the impending flight. A Pennsylvania Railroad express train from Jersey City was to guide the pilot from New York to Philadelphia and back. Clarence K. "Daredevil" Hamilton, a red-haired, jug-eared flier who had achieved considerable fame at the Los Angeles air show, was chosen as pilot.

The event soon became touted as a race between a train and a plane. Few Philadelphians expected the Farman biplane (brought from Los Angles), a twenty-five-horsepower-propelled muslin kite to keep up with a powerful locomotive. Hamilton's route was to enter the City of Philadelphia over Torresdale and then follow the Pennsylvania Railroad tracks through Holmesburg, Tacony, Wissinoming and Frankford before landing on a specially prepared field at Front and Erie Avenues. Each of these communities prepared themselves for the day of the flight. Many schools scheduled late openings, housewives postponed chores and work in the Northeast came to a halt.

On June 13, 1910, the flight began at Governor's Island, where Governor Charles Evans Hughes of New York gave Hamilton a letter for Governor Edwin S. Stuart of Pennsylvania prior to the 7:36 a.m. departure time. The plane had little difficulty staying close to the train. Approximately one million people lined the Pennsylvania Railroad route. Local newspapers in Northeast Philadelphia commented that no one was in the communities of Bustleton, Somerton, Holmesburg and Tacony because all were down at the train tracks, waiting to see Hamilton in the Farman biplane pass by about 9:15 a.m. In Torresdale, at the railroad tracks near Linden Avenue, a crowd

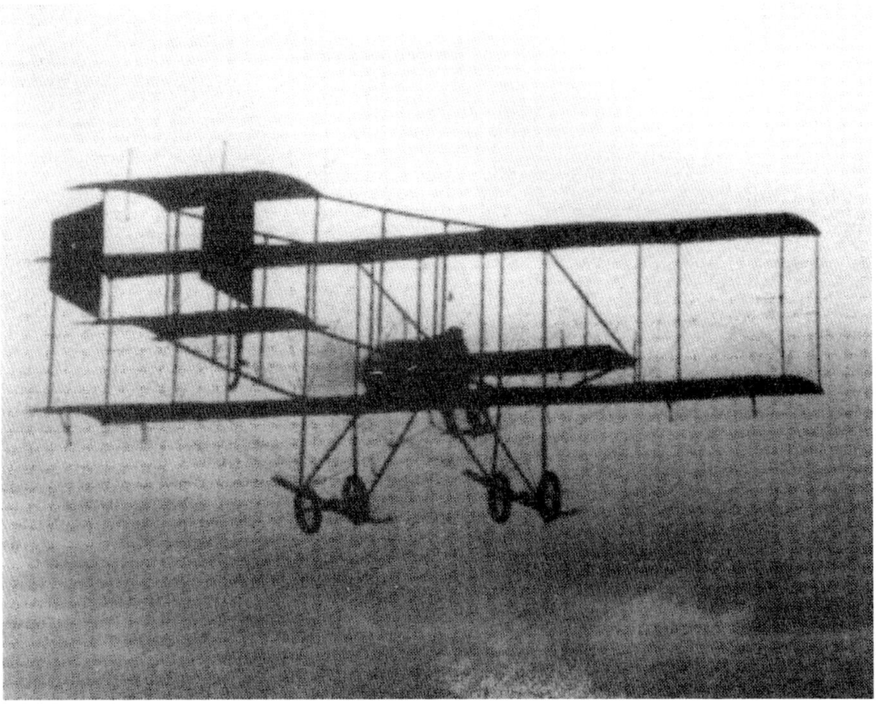

The Farman biplane flies over Philadelphia in 1910. During Clarence Hamilton's flight, over one million people saw the plane on June 13, 1910.

of 500 gathered; at Holmesburg station at State Road, there was another crowd of 1,000; and at Tacony station at Longshore east of Keystone Street, there were over 1,500. Over 2,000 people from Frankford headed to the Front and Erie landing field site.

Spectators began arriving at the field at 6:30 a.m., and by 7:00 a.m. the slopes on the border of the field were filled. People were on the roofs of a nearby farmhouse and residences on Erie Avenue. By 9:00 a.m. the crowd had grown to 100,000. At 9:36 a.m. a great shout went up from the crowd. Hamilton had landed safely, setting a new record for nonstop distance flown by a plane. Five minutes later, the train arrived on the nearby railroad tracks. Throughout the flight, Hamilton's wife had ridden on the rear platform of the train to encourage her husband. Embracing him afterward, she called the flight "wonderful." The 86-mile trip took one hour and fifty-one minutes, averaging 46.92 miles per hour. The highest speed was 75 miles per hour.

Holmesburg was honored to have Arthur T. Atherholt of the Holmesburg Improvement Association, a noted balloonist of the day, greet the pilot. To Atherholt, it was "the most perfect landing I have ever seen." Hamilton told the crowd, "The train could not match me for speed. I slowed down to allow them to catch up with me. I needed the train to give me proper directions." Governor Stuart of Pennsylvania, there to welcome the pilot, remarked:

> *My friends you have just witnessed a great sight today. A peep into what the future might hold for your children has been offered to you. Some day it is likely that the air will be filled with machines such as that which you have just seen. A great era is at hand. I am proud to be here, and was proud to shake the hand of the man who accomplished such a feat as flying from New York to Philadelphia.*

Hamilton went off to lunch at the Majestic Hotel on Broad Street while mechanics checked his plane. The train was sent to North Philadelphia Station to be turned around for the return trip. A thousand policemen, many on horseback, restrained the crowd from touching the biplane. Hamilton returned to the plane to wait for the train that was to guide him. Impatient, Hamilton decided not to wait and took off at 11:23 a.m. without it. People from Tacony, Holmesburg and Torresdale who had chosen to stay by the Pennsylvania Railroad tracks were treated to the unobstructed sight of the Farman biplane. The train, which left five minutes after Hamilton, raced at seventy-five miles per hour, catching the plane at Lawrenceville, New Jersey. A forced landing in Perth Amboy, New Jersey, delayed Hamilton's return flight, but a new propeller blade brought to him by his crew allowed for his return to Governor's Island at 6:41 p.m.

Pride filled much of the conversations of Northeast Philadelphians for weeks following the world-changing event. Arthur Atherholt's close friend, world-famous balloonist Samuel A. King, remarked, "I've seen some great ballooning in my day, but this flight means that ballooning days are done. Air planes offer the greatest opportunity to improved air flights." Newspapers carried headlines like "Airplane Outstrips Locomotive in Mad Race Across New Jersey on Homeward Trip." Ironically, the airplane was not an American-built Wright brothers plane, but a French-built Farman biplane. Few seemed to care. Northeast Philadelphians had seen air flight, and it was invented by Americans. So special was the event that the *New York Times*'s front page included an artist's sketch of Hamilton, and the *Philadelphia Public Ledger* promised its readers a full two-page copperplate pictorial of the flight as a souvenir. Few events in the history of Northeast Philadelphia can surpass the excitement of June 13, 1910.

PHOTOGRAPHY AND MOTION PICTURE CONNECTIONS TO NORTHEAST PHILADELPHIA

On first consideration, the development of photography and motion pictures would seem to have little to do with Northeast Philadelphia. In the early years of these technologies, the Northeast was a farming region removed from city life and isolated from its activities. Nevertheless, two men with ties to Northeast Philadelphia, Robert Cornelius (1809–1893) and Siegmund Lubin (1851–1923), made major contributions to the development of visual images from 1839 to 1915. Cornelius had a summer home on Frankford Avenue in what is now Wissinoming Park, while Lubin, who never lived in the Northeast, used it as background in over thirty of his movies. In writing the history of Northeast Philadelphia, it is difficult to leave these men out, since both contributed much to our culture and lifestyle.

Previous to 1839, photography was unknown. In August of that year, French scientist Louis Daguerre (1787–1851) announced the discovery of a process of getting a picture on a copperplate by using light from the sun. His discovery startled the world and brought him great fame. He was even granted a life pension by the French government for his work.

Before any photographs from Europe reached America, however, Philadelphia inventor Joseph Saxton duplicated Daguerre's feat by taking a picture of Central High School on September 25, 1839, with a camera made from a cigar box, an ordinary burning glass, a piece of polished silver ribbon and some flashes of iodine. Both Saxton and Daguerre's techniques required an hour and a half of exposure time to get a picture

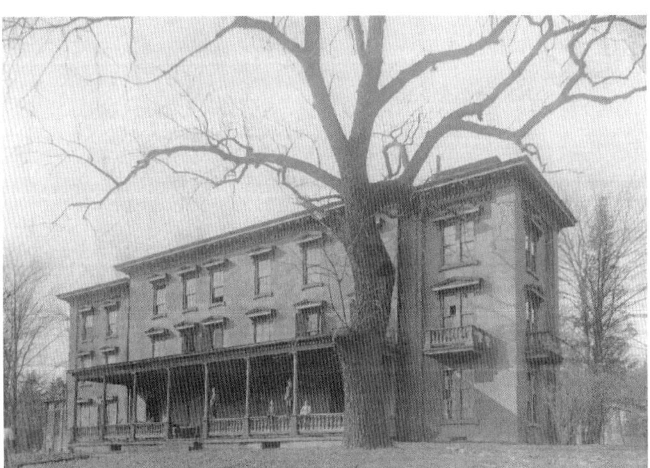

Robert Cornelius's house near Frankford Avenue on the top of a hill in what is today Wissinoming Park. Cornelius, who took the first portrait of a human face in 1839, planted many trees from around the world on his estate. The house was torn down at the beginning of the twentieth century.

on the copperplate. It would seem that this process could be used only for objects, not portraits of people.

Robert Cornelius was a metallurgist and a member of the Franklin Institute, where he had met and worked with Saxton to learn the basis of Daguerre's process. Cornelius brought with him a strong practical knowledge of metallurgy and chemistry. He experimented with photographic chemistry in search of a reagent to accelerate the process. Using iodine and the reagent bromine, he was able to decrease exposure time down to one minute. He took his first picture, a self portrait, using his new process outside his business office at Eighth and Market Streets in the fall of 1839. In the now-famous photograph, his image is poorly centered, which he explained by saying, "Being alone, I ran in front of the camera and could not know until the picture was taken that I had not stood directly opposite the center of the lens." Yet Cornelius had the distinction of having taken the first portrait of a human face with a camera. A month later, when the first daguerreotypes reached America, they were found to be inferior to Cornelius's picture.

Paul Beck Goddard of the University of Pennsylvania, who was the first to use bromide to accelerate the development of pictures, formed a partnership with Cornelius, and they operated a photographic studio in Philadelphia in the 1840s. Portraits using Cornelius's improved cameras were taken daily, "weather permitting."

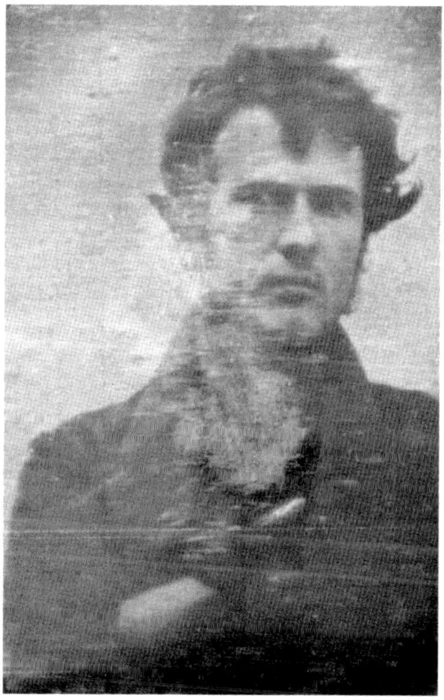

The original picture, a self-portrait, taken by Cornelius in 1839. On the back of this daguerreotype, he wrote: "The first picture ever taken, 1839." In reality it was the first portrait of a human being ever taken.

Cornelius's professional studios mushroomed into the hundreds, making him a rich man. Like many wealthy Philadelphians, he sought a summer home outside the city. He bought over one hundred acres on the east side of Bristol Pike (now Frankford Avenue) in Wissinoming and built a home at the top of a hill overlooking a spring lake near where Comly Street is today. Having sufficient wealth, he either lost interest in photography or realized that he could make even more money running his newly formed gas and lighting company, which he did for the next half century. He supplied much of the illumination for Philadelphia's 1876 Centennial Exposition. His hobby throughout this period was his summer home in Wissinoming, which he sought to beautify. As he traveled throughout the world, he purchased over 150 trees for planting there. It was rumored that some of the trees that he brought back were so large that they extended beyond the boat, front to back. Cornelius died in 1893 at the age of eighty-four and was honored as one of Philadelphia's leading citizens. Eventually the Cornelius estate was purchased by the city on January 9, 1913, as recommended by the Art Jury, a conservationist group, "because of its many valuable trees." The house was torn down as part of the Art Jury's plan for the park. The lake was removed by closing off the natural springs, but many of the trees brought to America by Cornelius can still to be found in the park.

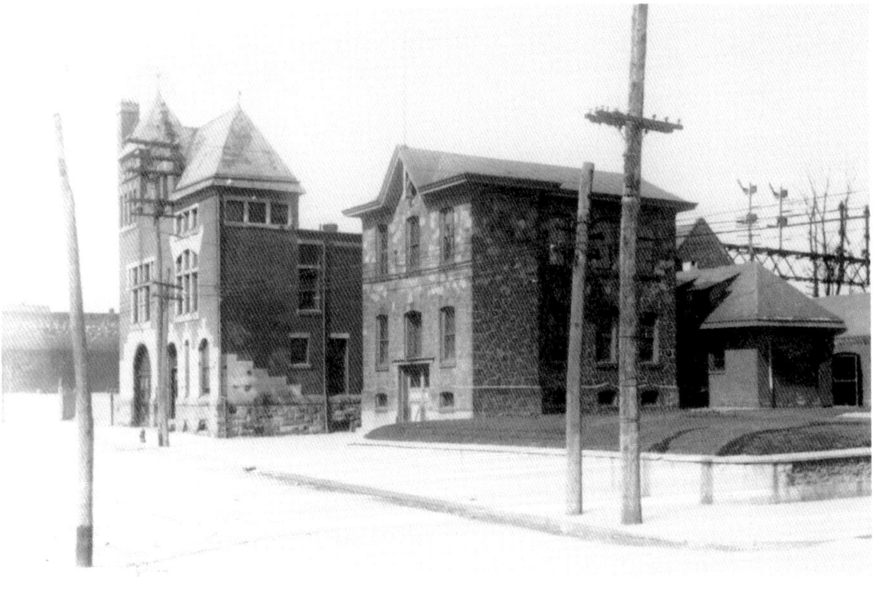

A picture of the Tacony Fire House, which responded to the fire that Lubin started at the Tacony Iron Works on McGee Street and State Road.

The same year that Cornelius was lauded for his work at the 1876 exposition, a German-Jewish immigrant arrived in Philadelphia seeking employment. Siegmund Lubin went from job to job until he found work in the emerging motion picture industry. By 1904, he was producing one-reel fiction movies every month, often with large doses of kissing and romance. In 1910, he built in Philadelphia what was then America's most up-to-date glass-structured film studio. Most of his movies had a distinctive Philadelphia flavor since they were shot on location throughout the city. Some of the earliest films he ever made were produced in Northeast Philadelphia. The Holmesburg Scrapbook Collection, compiled by Librarian Katherine M. Petty from 1911 to 1948, contains six accounts of the Lubin production company making western films in Pennypack Park near Holmesburg. It was not unusual to see actors dressed in cowboy and Indian costumes riding on horses at Rhawn Street and Frankford Avenue. Many citizens of Holmesburg, Tacony and Frankford were cast as extras in Lubin's movies. He didn't pay for extras, but he always had an excess of volunteers. The horse paths along Pennypack Creek were among Lubin's favorite spots for cowboy and Indian chases. He could take a ground shot and then use the Rhawn Street Bridge for shots from above. The old barns and mills along the creek provided other scenery that might be needed. Besides Holmesburg, Lubin also produced movies that included a scene at the Seven Stars Tavern and chases along Oxford Avenue, both in Frankford. He also produced the film *Fortune Hunter* in Bustleton. In all, Lubin made more than thirty silent movies in various parts of the Northeast. Unfortunately, these films showing the old sights of the area were destroyed in an unexpected explosion in Lubin's film library on June 13, 1914. The explosion also helped put Lubin out of business, since he made much of his money renting these films to theatres.

Another disturbing incident in Lubin's filmmaking career also occurred in 1914, when he was making the movie thriller *Gods of Fate* in Tacony. Lubin was setting up a scene showing a building on fire and his male hero rescuing a damsel in distress. The Tacony Iron Works, where the William Penn statue that sits atop city hall had been cast in the 1880s, had been vacant since 1909, when the company went out of business. After assuring the owners that the fire would be extinguished without substantial damage to the property, Lubin received permission to use the building for his film. On the day of the filming, a small group of people, mostly youths, gathered to watch. Lubin was in his director's chair as the actors assumed their places, the girl in the building at a window and the male lead outside. Lubin called for action and the fire was started in the building. Lubin was visibly pleased, as the actors played out the rescue scene as directed. When the scene was over, however, the building was

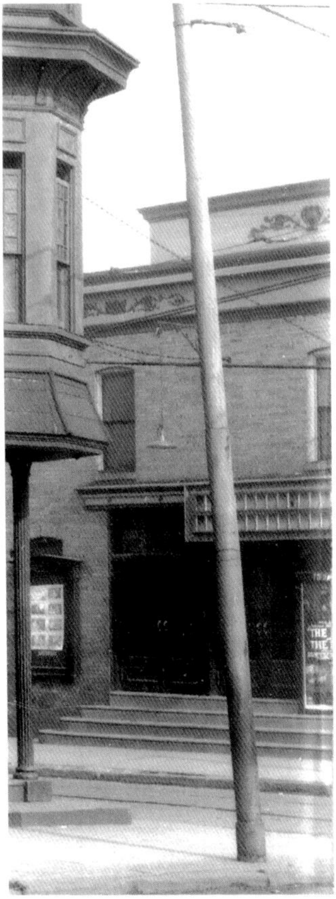

A view from Richmond Street of the New Elm Movie House on Bridge Street. The movie house featured silent films from 1910 to 1918 with a piano background. Charles D. Silcox was among the early piano players at the movie house.

immersed in flames. Extras tried to extinguish the fire but could not—it was out of control. A fire alarm was pulled and the fire company from four blocks away on Longshore Street responded. Needless to say, they were not pleased, as the Disston lumberyard was just across the street. If that had caught on fire, all of Disston Saw Company might have burned to the ground. Word quickly spread throughout the town that the Disston factory was in danger. The fireman, now surrounded by hundreds of workers and people of the community, decided to let the old Tacony Iron Works building burn to the ground and focus on preventing the Disston lumberyard from catching on fire. Afterward, the town leaders were so upset that they barred Lubin from making any more pictures in Tacony. Siegmund Lubin, although somewhat of a scoundrel and an unethical salesman, was the one most responsible for Northeast Philadelphia's participation in the early motion picture industry.

The last report of the Lubin Film Company making motion pictures in Holmesburg appeared in the *Frankford Dispatch* on May 12, 1916. Filming in

Holmesburg and nearly bankrupt, Lubin took pictures of the Boy Scouts at Crystal Field in all their drills and contests, caught Fire Company No. 36 coming out of the firehouse and followed them, taking pictures of them extinguishing the fire. The "Tom Thumb Wedding" that had caused so much interest at the Presbyterian church was also filmed. Later in the same week, all of these motion pictures were shown at the open-air theatre at Crystal Field (Rowland Avenue and Rhawn Street) with all of Holmesburg coming out to see them. These motion pictures were never destroyed and might still be stored in some attic of an old house in Holmesburg.

Northeast Photographer: The William Sliker Collection, 1900–1967

One of the best collections of the sights of Northeast Philadelphia in the years between 1905 and 1939 is from William H. Sliker Photo and Arts Studio, located at 4745 Mercer Street in Bridesburg. The studio was opened in 1900 by William Sliker and his wife Ann, who had recently arrived from Germany. Bridesburg at the time had a large number of German residents, which made Sliker's heritage a valuable asset in establishing the business.

When the business began, Sliker was a studio photographer working out of the first floor of the Mercer Street studio. The front room of the house was a sitting or waiting room for the many families and individuals that came to the studio for family portraits. The back room on the first floor of the house was where pictures were taken. It contained ten to twelve different backdrops that depicted a forest, a chapel, a picture of the Delaware River

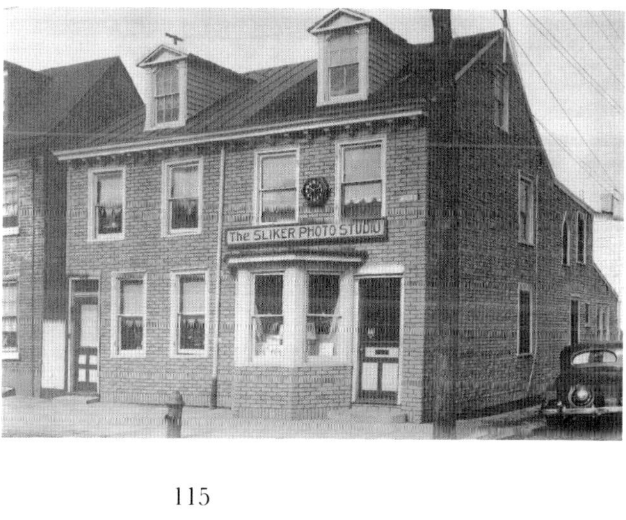

The Sliker Photo Studio in Bridesburg in the 1930s.

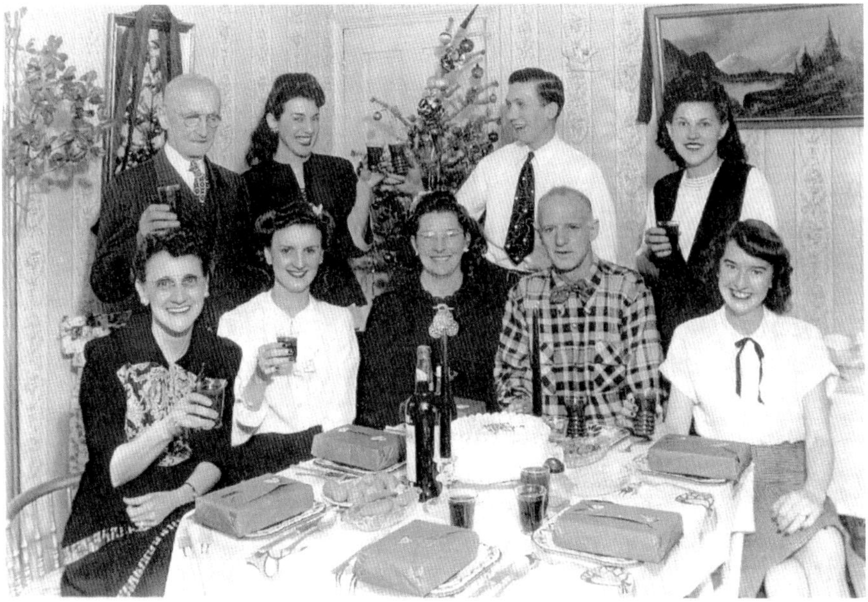

Sliker Studio staff 1946 Christmas party with gifts given to every employee. William Sliker is standing in the back row on the left with his son, Roy Sliker, seated between workers Amanda and Dorothy Omrod.

from the local Bridge Street dock, spring flowers and other artificial settings. This allowed Sliker to take wedding pictures, family portraits and individual pictures in many different settings in the same room. This was important because, at the time, he was using cameras with heavy glass plates that were cumbersome and easily broken in transit.

The two rooms on the second floor were set aside as darkrooms for developing pictures. In those days, pictures were developed from glass plates. When the new Eastman Kodak cameras became the rage throughout the country, Sliker began developing Kodak film. Through the use of a twelve-exposure roll of two-inch gelatin-coated paper film, a picture could be taken by almost anyone using a little boxlike camera. Developed by Eastman in the 1880s, the film was originally sent back to Rochester, New York, for developing. However, by 1910 Eastman was more interested in the selling of improved film than in developing film. This gave individual photography studios an opportunity to become major developers of the new Kodak film.

About the same time, Sliker's oldest son, Charles, began working in the shop with his father. William continued the studio work, but the seventeen-year-old Charles seized the opportunity presented by the new Kodak box camera to establish a pickup and delivery service at drugstores throughout Northeast

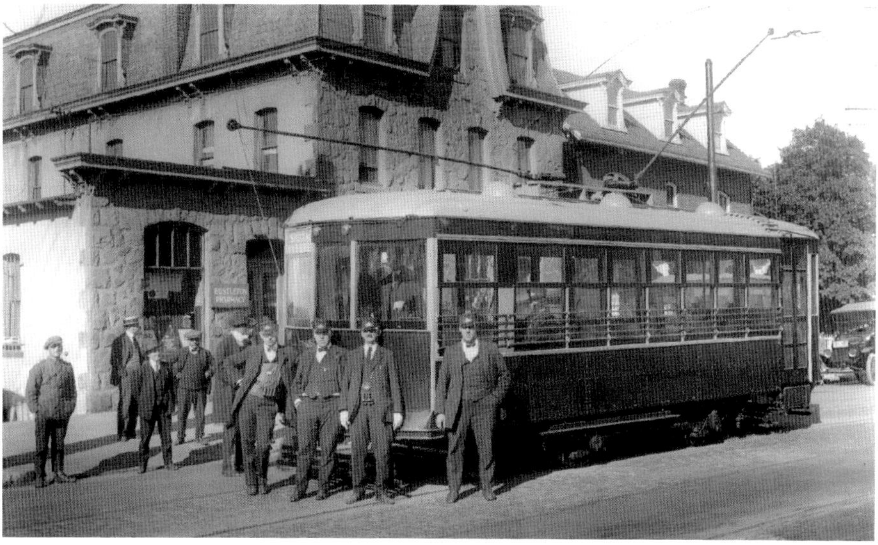

William Sliker was present at the first arrival of a trolley to Bustleton in November 1922.

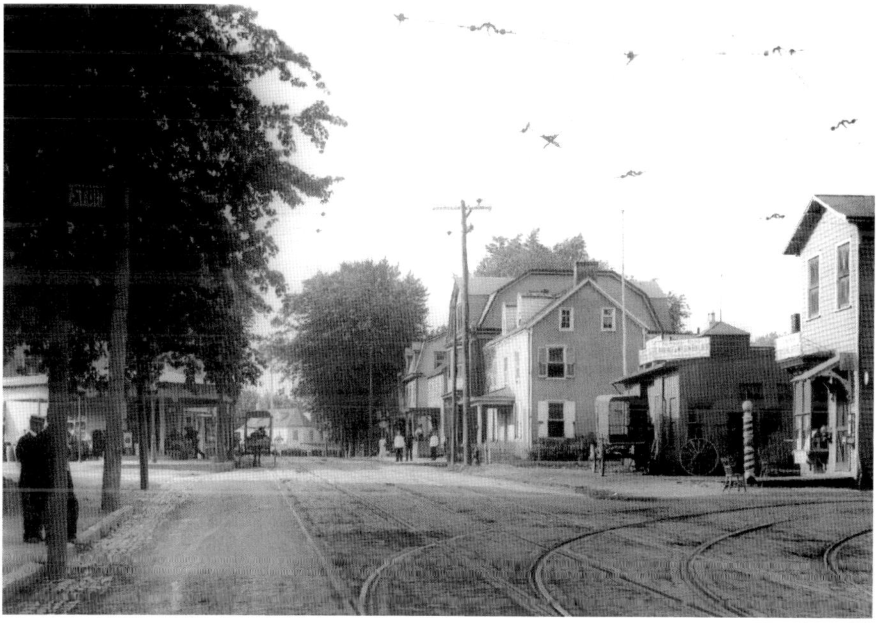

A Sliker photo of Second Street Pike in Fox Chase in 1918.

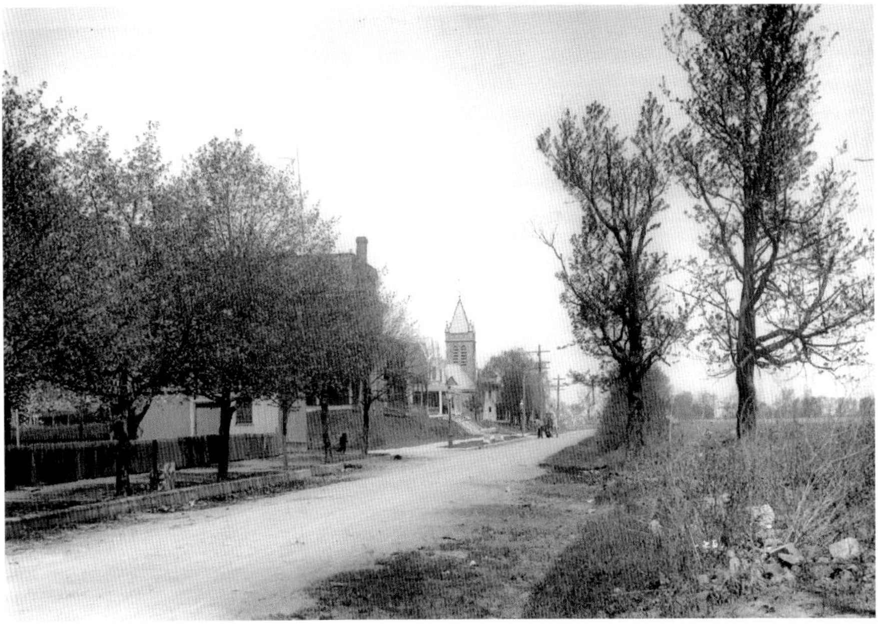

A Sliker photo of Tacony. This picture of Tyson Street shows that the street was the outer border of the town in the 1920s.

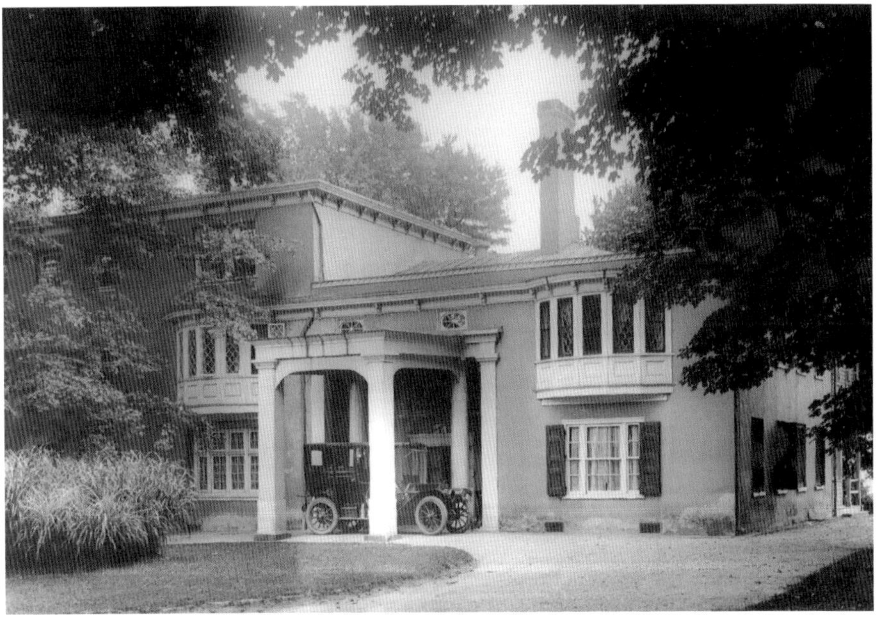

A Sliker photo of the Ury House in Fox Chase in 1915. The original structure was built by early settlers in 1682. The building was razed in 1973.

Philadelphia. He would set out on horseback three days a week, riding routes that included the communities of Frankford, Tacony, Bustleton, Wissinoming, Torresdale, Lawndale, Fox Chase, Burholme, Somerton, Byberry and Rockledge. Much of this ride was in open farm country, through forests and small villages. He would pick up film left at the general store or local pharmacy stores for developing, take it to the Bridesburg Studio, develop it and deliver the photographs to the stores on the same day the following week.

In all Charles had three routes that covered the area. A description of one remains in the Bridesburg Historical Society collection:

> *Charles rode up Bridge Street to Frankford Avenue then over Frankford Avenue to Holmesburg, turning right on Welsh rode to Feasterville and Southampton. He returned by coming down Second Street Pike, past the toll-gate at Rockledge, through Fox Chase and Burholme on the Oxford Pike to Frankford and then down Bridge Street to Bridesburg.*

It would take a full day to complete this one circuit of stores. When one considers that most of these roads were dirt and that rain and snow were always possibilities, this was a challenging a job for a young man. Clearly, Charles was making a positive impact on the profitability of the Sliker Studio.

Yet another opportunity presented itself as Charles increased his contacts with the store owners of the Northeast. They informed Charles that they had

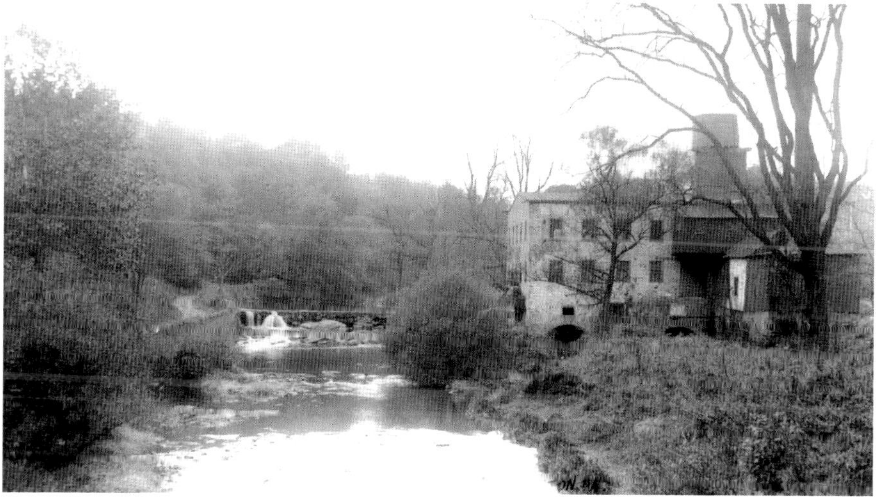

A Sliker photo of the La Grange cotton mill on Pennypack Creek near Bustleton in 1920.

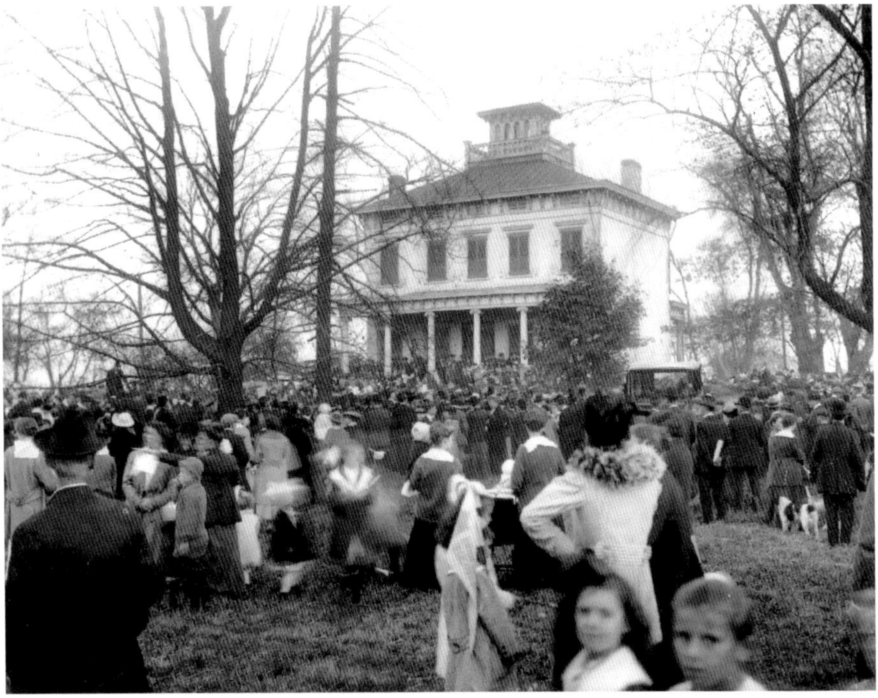

A Sliker photo of the dedication of Bridesburg Park on October 28, 1916.

numerous requests for picture postcards of the area. People wanted pictures of important area landmarks such as churches, schools, libraries, parks and historical taverns that they could send their friends and loved ones. The Sliker Studio produced such picture postcards in packages of twenty-five for each section of the Northeast. Many of these postcards are still available at postcard shows and sales throughout the country. They all have the same style—they focus on buildings, streets and institutions, not people, reflecting a time when man's accomplishments were embodied most in images that embraced the building of a permanent and civilized society.

The popularity of the postcards in the stores of the Northeast grew between 1905 and 1920. It was then that William and Charles were approached to take individual family postcard pictures. If you had a house, farm or business that you were particularly proud to own, you could order twenty postcards at a good price for your friends. These pictures of homes and families were not sold at local general stores; rather, they remained a status symbol for the wealth of the community. It is not clear as to who took what photograph since they all were stamped "Sliker Photographic and Art Studio." Since we do know that this family-operated business

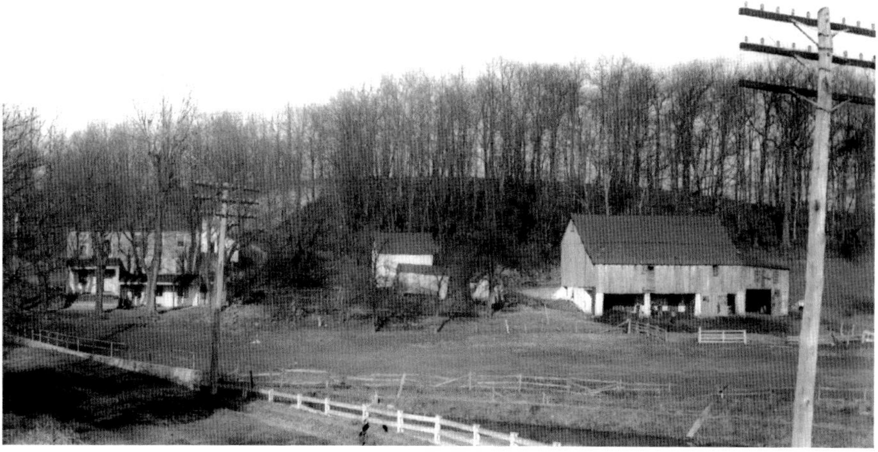

Sliker spent much of his time in the countryside of Northeast Philadelphia. This picture of a farm in Somerton shows early Bustleton Avenue.

averaged just five employees, we can assume that the pictures were taken by either William or his son Charles.

During the 1940s, the studio turned to school pictures for most of its business. It held the contract for pictures taken of Frankford High School and Harding Jr. High School students. This included pictures of dances, special school activities and sporting events. The business continued until William died in 1952. Charles cut back on services after his father's death, closing the studio in 1967. Charles died in 1968.

In 1997, approximately two hundred glass plate negatives from the Sliker Collection remained in the possession of Charles's son. It was at that time that Harry C. Silcox purchased the glass negatives and had his son Bruce reprint the pictures from the negatives. The pictures in this section are from the Sliker Collection of Photos from Northeast Philadelphia.

Appendix

The Origins of the Names of Northeast Philadelphia Neighborhoods

Most people in Northeast Philadelphia know little about how the major neighborhoods of the community got their names. Some are very old names dating back to the years prior to the founding of the nation, while other names developed in recent times. The enclosed list gives some idea of how Northeast Philadelphia neighborhoods received their names.

Bridesburg

A community founded by German immigrants in the early 1700s at the mouth of the Frankford Creek and the Delaware River. Its purpose was to provide a river port for the growing industrial village of Frankford. The wharves at the end of Bridge Street were the center for town activity in the early years. The bridge over Frankford Creek provided a direct street link to Frankford called Bridge Street. The village used a ferry across Frankford Creek to get to the town of Frankford. At first, Joseph Kirkbride operated a ferry before the bridge was built. This resulted in the village being called Kirkbridesburg. Later it was shortened to Bridesburg.

Burholme

Outstanding among the residents in the area was the Ryerss family. Their home near what is now Cottman and Rising Sun Avenues was called Burholme, named in honor of the family's ancestral home in England. After

Ryerss's death and in accordance with his will, the property was given to the city to be used as a community park. The beautiful mansion became a museum and library. According to the will, the seventy acres of rolling lawns and gardens were to be open to the public. After the Ryerss estate became city property, those living in what was then called Five Points held a public meeting and voted to change the name of their community to Burholme.

BUSTLETON

The area with the most stories as to how it got its name is Bustleton. One thing is for sure: it was one of the area's early trading centers. How it got its name remains a mystery. You choose the story you like.

Historian S.F. Hotchkin, writing in his book *York Road Old and New, Fox Chase, Bustleton*, cites that many people in the area came from an English town called Brislington. Early spelling was Busselton, which was later shortened to Bustleton. Hotchkin also cites a second legend that noted that the passage of Revolutionary War soldiers on their way to Crooked Billet (Hatboro) made a bustling (Bustleton) place of the village. A third story by Reverend S.F. Hotchkin was that a very busy housewife who became known as "Bustling Bess" lived near the railroad station, and passengers suggested naming the station Bustleton in her honor.

A fourth story told by the black community was that Cyrus Bustill, an African American, had a bakery in the small town south of Smithville (Somerton) in the 1770s. He married a woman from the local Indian tribe. When George Washington's army was on the march to Princeton to do battle with the German Hessians, they stopped at Bustill's bakery for bread. Washington gave Bustill a gold coin for his services. This became a well-known story in the town, and it was not long before its name became Bustleton. The Bustill family moved to Philadelphia after 1800 and soon became active members of Philadelphia's African American community

BYBERRY

Byberry was first settled by the four Walton brothers—Nathaniel, Thomas, Daniel and William—from Bibury, England. They settled the area in 1675, living for the first six months in caves without houses. The name Byberry was taken from the town they came from in England. The area was settled by the Quakers, who owned farms or lived in one of three local areas: Mechanicsville, Byberry and Smithville. The Byberry Friends was established in 1683 and the nearby Quaker school in 1710. In 1854, there was great debate in the region as to whether Byberry should remain in the city or become part of Bucks County. Led by Robert Purvis, Byberry elected to stay in Philadelphia.

FOX CHASE

The Fox Chase Inn was originally started in 1705 as a log cabin; then it was replaced by a fine colonial hotel that was once the glory of the Fox Chase village. The village soon adopted the hotel's name. At the time, Fox Chase catered to the elite who came in coach-and-fours or on horseback to engage in fox hunting. Many visitors to the numerous mansions in the vicinity also stayed here. Betsy Ross stopped there on her way to visit her sister in Jenkintown. Many distinguished visitors to the Ury House were also guests in the Fox Chase Inn.

FRANKFORD

Frankford was sold by William Penn as a twenty-thousand-acre parcel to the Society of Free Traders, a group of London businessmen. Penn purchased the Swedish gristmill of two-hundred acres from Lasse Cock and his brother for the Society of Free Traders. The land purchased was known as the Manor of Frank, from which Frankford derived its name. The principal purchasers of the Manor of Frank were Thomas Fairman, Henry Waddy, Robert Adam and Thomas Seary. Fairman was Penn's lieutenant. He was living in Shackamaxon when Penn arrived in America. Penn requested that Fairman establish a Quaker meeting in Frankford. The first Frankford meeting was held at the home of Sarah Seary in July 1683.

HOLMESBURG

Holmesburg is one of the oldest sections north of Oxford Township. Located on the King's Highway (Frankford Avenue), it was one of the early stagecoach stops for travelers going to New York or Boston. The bridge over the Pennypack in Holmesburg dates back to 1697. The town's name prior to 1801 was Washingtonville, but it was renamed Holmesburg, taking its name from John Holme, who about that time purchased a great deal of land and established a lumberyard first called the Washington Lumber Yard and afterward changed to Holme Lumber Yard. John Holme may have been related to Thomas Holme, the surveyor general for William Penn, but no proof of kinship has ever been established. The name Holmes is probably just an interesting coincidence.

Lawncrest

Until 1950 the name Lawncrest did not exist. It was used by the City of Philadelphia to unify two district neighborhoods, Crescentville and Lawndale, when the Lawncrest Recreation Center and Lawncrest Library were built. Crescentville took its name from the Crescent Factory, a rope mill that operated there in the 1800s. In the late 1800s, the Lawndale Land Company developed homes in the northern region of the community named Lawndale. Through the center of Crescentville and Lawndale ran its only major road, which originally was an old American Indian trail and was later named Second Street Pike. Today it is Rising Sun Avenue.

Mayfair

How Mayfair got its name is uncertain. Some say it was the original telephone exchange. Others say that local civic leader Thomas Donahue (3521 Aldine Street) gave the community its name in 1928, when he declared at a community meeting that "we 'may fair' well if we get behind this community and push—so why not call it Mayfair?" Whichever story is true, it is clear that the opening of the Mayfair Movie House in 1936 and the organization of the store owners adjacent to the area into the Mayfair Businessmen's Association cemented the name to the community.

Pennypack Creek

The name Pennypack is derived from the Lenni-Lenape word meaning "deep dead water, water without much current." Before William Penn, the Swedish settlers called the area by many variations of that name. However, on Surveyor General Thomas Holme's plan of the Philadelphia area in 1681, it is called Dublin Creek, and on a later map it is called Dublin

River. Nevertheless, in 1701 Penn reverted back to using the Indian word "Pemmapecka" when discussing the area. This was the name embraced after 1701, and the creek became known by the English word Pennypack.

SOMERTON

The area now referred to as "Somerton" started out as the township of Byberry and Moreland. The territory was settled in 1645 by the Swedes and later in 1682 by Quakers. A small village grew up around a store and blacksmith shop and was called Smithfield. Smithfield remained on local maps until after the Civil War, when a post office was opened and named in honor of Judge Sommers of the District Court and a resident of the town. The post office soon became known as Somerton, as did the town.

TACONY

Before the Europeans arrived, Tacony was home to the Toaconick Indians, a tribe of the Lenni-Lenape. They lived along the banks of the Quessionwonmick River, now known as Frankford Creek. The area had yet a second creek, called the Tacony Creek, that ran northeast of Frankford. The section was referred to as "Tookany." Tacony got its name from the Indian tribe and the creek.

TORRESDALE

In an article written in 1933 by Alfred M. Townson, Torresdale is described as the site of an Indian village named Poquessing. It was later named Risdon's Ferry because it was a delivery point for Delaware River mail and passenger service for the Philadelphia–Trenton daily boats. It was a happy and fashionable place in the period after the Civil War, when the local citizens comprised the leading Philadelphia families like the Fitlers, Biddles, Drexels, Middletons, Phillips and Carsons.

Charles Macalester settled on the riverfront in the year 1850 and became a large landowner and later named the settlement Torresdale after his hunting lodge in Scotland. He later built and lived in Glengarry, named after his Scottish home. When William Foerderer purchased Glengarry, he kept the "Glen" and added the first part of his last name, so it became Glen Foerd.

Verreeville

Veree Mills was built in the 1650s on what today would be the west side of Verree Road between Susquehanna and Bloomfield Roads. The estate was owned by the Verree family during the eighteenth and nineteenth centuries. The area was soon named Verreeville after the Verree family. They were of French descent, the original name being Verrier. The Ury House was the most famous structure in Verreeville. The house was constructed by Swedish settlers who arrived in 1645. The blockhouse was for protection from the Lenni-Lenape Indians. Located on a sixty-acre estate, it became the centerpiece of Verreeville. The house remained one of the oldest in Northeast Philadelphia until it was torn down in 1973.

Wissinoming

The area was named "Quessmacemink" in the first land grant given to a Swedish settler named Peter Cook in 1675. The alternate spelling of this name is Kwissinomink, which was pronounced "Wissinoming" in English, meaning "Duck Creek." In 1805, a survey was made of Howell Farm, the land on which much of Wissinoming is built. Howell Farm comprised two hundred acres of land bounded on the east by what is today Torresdale Avenue, on the west by Wissinoming Park (Cornelius Mansion), on the north by Wissinoming Creek (Robbins Avenue area) and on the south by Dark Run Lane (Cheltenham Avenue). The Howell Farm was purchased by the Wissinoming Land Company in 1886, which was composed of Fishtown textile workers who sought homes in the country for their children. The oldest Wissinoming industry was the cordage works of E.H. Fitler on Tacony Street, founded by former Philadelphia mayor Edwin H. Fitler in 1864.